Enjoy the walks and may I wish you -

Happy Walking!

Happy walking! John N. Merrill

Shinrin-Yoku

- The healing art of Japanese Forest bathing.

I have quite naturally, been doing this all my life on my walks. By simply going for a walk, on my own, brings huge benefits, not just breathing in clean fresh air but getting exercise and connecting with the sacred world around us. We are connected to and one with everything. The only way to appreciate and deeply understand nature and all its beauty and wonder is by being alone.....quite simply miracles occur.

Walk peacefully through a wood and just observe the leaves, the berries, the way a tree grows, the flowers that carpet the floor. Stop, sit and listen to the bird song, or watch a squirrel rooting among the leaves. By being still and observant many other animals and features come into view. Sit at the base of tree and feel its strength and wisdom. Sit by a tinkling stream and observe the wildlife that inhabits this domain. Lie on the ground and gaze at the sky and watch the clouds pass over, or at night the whole cosmos becomes visible. Find an old oak tree and give it a hug. Communicate with the birds, they will sing back to you and hop onto other branches to get a clearer view. Talk to the flowers, caress their leaves and admire their delicate design and smell their fragrance. If you feel hungry eat some wild blackberries. The natural world has much to teach us and enlivens our soul getting back to the basics of life. Return home refreshed and invigorated and go about your day with more vigour, purpose and energy. Then after a few days go back again and rejuvenate your being.

www.shinrin-yoku.org
(Revd. John N. Merrill - February 2019).

The Art of walking the John Merrill Way.

1. Always set off in the clothes you plan to wear all day, given the weather conditions. Only on sudden changes in the weather will I stop and put on a waterproof or warmer clothing.

2. Set off at a steady comfortable pace, which you can maintain all day. You should end the walk as fresh as when you started.

3. Maintain your pace and don't stop. Stopping for any period of time disrupts your rythmn and takes upwards of a mile (20 mins) to settle back down into the flow/ease of movement.

4. Switch your phone off. Listen and enjoy the countryside - the smell of the flowers, bird song, the rustle of leaves and the tinkling stream, and observe the wildlife.

5. Ignore the mileage and ascents - don't tick the miles or hills, just concentrate on what the walk's goal is. To think otherwise slows you down and makes the walk a struggle rather than a joy. In a similar vein, when ascending just keep a steady pace and keep going. To stop is to disrupt the flow and make the ascent interminable.

6. Whist a walk is a challenge to complete, it is not just exercise. You should enjoy the world around you, the flowers, birds, wildlife and nature and look at and explore the historical buildings and churches that you pass. Industrial complex's have their own beauty. All are part of life's rich tapestry.

7. Remember that for every mile you walk, you extend your life by 21 minutes.

8. A journey of a 1,000 miles begins with a single step and a mile requires 2,000 strides.

"The expert traveller leaves no footprints" Lao Tzu.

A pause for thought ....
The Ten Indian Commandments -

1. Treat the earth and all that dwell thereon with respect.

2. Remain close to the Great Spirt.

3. Show great respect for your fellow beings.

4. Work together for the benefit of all mankind.

5. Give assistance and kindness wherever needed.

6. Do what you know to be right.

7. Look after the well-being of mind and body.

8. Dedicate a share of your efforts to the greater good.

9. Be truthful and honest at all times.

10. Take full responsibility for your actions.

Other Canal Walk Guides by Revd. John N. Merrill

Derbyshire & Nottinghamshire - 30 walks. - Erewash, Derby, Trent & Mersey, Nottingham, Beeston & Nutbrook Canals.
Short Circular Walks on the Canals of South Yorkshire.
Cheshire & Staffordshire - 40 walks. - Peak Forest, Macclesfield, Caldon, & Trent & Mersey Canals.
Staffordshire - 36 walks. - Trent & Mersey, Coventry, & Staffordshire & Worcestershire Canals.
Walking the Cheshire Ring - 100 miles.
The Grantham Canal - 15 walks.
Walking the Trent & Mersey Canal - 100 miles.
Walking Llangollen Canal - 50 miles.
Walking the Derby Canal Ring - 28 miles.
The Salt & Sails Trail - 20 miles - River Weaver Navigation.
Short circular walks on the Chesterfield Canal - 22 walks.
Short Circular walks on the Cromford Canal - 10 walks.
Short Circular Walks on the River Lee Navigation - Northern volume - 10 walks.
Short Circular Walks on the River Lee Navigation - Southern volume - 12 walks.
Walking the River Lee Navigation - 20 walks.
Short circular walks on the River Stort Navigation - 8 walks.
Walking the Canals of London - Regent's Canal, Grand Union Canal - 12 walks.
Short Circular walks in the Colne Valley - 8 walks - The Grand Union Canal.
The Blackwater and Chelmer Navigation.
Walking the River Wey & Godalming Navigation.
Walking the Grand Union Canal - 153 miles - London to Birmingham.
Walking the Oxford Canal - 85 miles.

Illustrated lectures
by
John N. Merrill

Lectures on
his major walks are available.
For further information
and bookings,
write to John Merrill at

THE JOHN MERRILL FOUNDATION
32, Holmesdale,
Waltham Cross,
Hertfordshire
EN8 8QY
England

Tel/Fax 01992 - 762776
e-mail - marathonhiker@aol.com
www.johnmerrillwalkguides.com

Illustrated Lectures include -

"Walking my Way" - Why I walk and some of walks I have done - a hilarious but exhausting talk, from more than 182,000 miles of walking!

"Walking Chesopeake and Ohio Canal" - 250 miles from Washington D.C. to Cumberland, Maryland, USA.

"North to Santiago via Fatima" - 650 mile pilgrim's walk to Santiago de Compostelo, through Portugal.

"Follow the blue blaze" - Walking around the Buckeye Trail in Ohio, USA. 1,300 miles - the first person to walk the complete trail in one continuous walk.

" WALKING AROUND LONDON" - a brief look at walking in the city and countryside around London, some 1,400 miles of walking. - Capital Ring, Canals, London Loop,River Thames, New River, Pymmes Brook Trail & Jubilee Walkway.

"Promoting walking, Pilgrimages, and understanding the countryside."

Short Circular Walks on the Canals of Derbyshire & Nottinghamshire

by Revd. John N. Merrill

THE CANAL WALKS SERIES - Vol. 1.

"Hiking the sacred paths & trails of the world for others to enjoy".

THE JOHN MERRILL FOUNDATION

THE JOHN MERRILL FOUNDATION
32, Holmesdale, Waltham Cross, Hertfordshire, England. EN8 8QY
Tel/Fax - 01992-762776
E-mail - john@johnmerrillwalkguides.co.uk
www. johnmerrillwalkguides.co.uk
www.thejohnmerrillministry.co.uk
www.londoninterfaithchurch.co.uk

A catalogue record for this book is available from the British Library.

Conceived, edited, typset and designed by *The John Merrill Foundation*
Printed and handmade by ***John N. Merrill.***
Book layout and cover design by ***John N. Merrill***

ISBN 978 - 1-903627-53-3
First Published - April 2004. Reprinted and revised - April 2013.
Special limited edition.

Typeset in Humanst521 - bold, italic, and plain 11pt, 14pt and 18pt
Main titles in 18pt .**Humanst521 Bd BT** by John Merrill in Adobe Pagemaker on a iMac.

Please note - *The maps in this guide are purely illustrative. You are encouraged to use the appropriate 1:25,000 O.S. Explorer map as detailed on each walk.*

John Merrill confirms he has walked all the routes in this book and detailed what he found. Meticulous research has been undertaken to ensure that this publication is highly accurate at the time of going to press. The publishers, however, cannot be held responsible for alterations, errors, omissions, or for changes in details given. They would welcome information to help keep the book up to date.

Photographs by Revd. John N. Merrill.

The John Merrill Foundation maintains the John Merrill Library and archives and administers the worldwide pubishing rights of John Merrill's works in all media formats.

Printed on paper from a 100% sustainable forest.
The John Merrill Foundation plants sufficient trees through the Woodland Trust to replenish the trees used in its publications.

John high up the mountain path, beside the Santa Barbara Chapel, overlooking Lake Garda, Italy.

A little about Revd. John N. Merrill

John is unique, possessing the skills of a marathon runner, mountain climber and athlete. Since his first 1,000 mile walk through the islands of the Inner and Outer Hebrides in 1970, he has since walked over 218,000 miles and worn out 132 pairs of boots, 49 rucksacks and more than 1,600 pairs of socks. He has brought marathon walking to Olympic standard. In 1978 he became the first person to walk around the entire coastline of Britain - 7,000 miles. He has walked across Europe, the Alps and Pyrenees - 3,000 miles with 600,000 feet of ascent and descent. In America he has walked the 2,500 mile Appalachian Trail; the Pacific Crest Trail - 2,500 miles in record time; the Continental Divide Trail; became the first person to thru-hike the Buckeye Trail - 1,350 miles in Ohio and completed a unique 4,260 mile walk in 178 days coast to coast across America. He has climbed all the mountains in New Mexico and walked all the trails.

In Britain he has walked all the National Trails many times; linked all the National Parks and trails in a 2,060 mile walk; completed a 1,608 mile Land's End to John o' Groats walk and countless other unique walks. He has walked three times to Santiago de Compostella via different routes; to St. Olav's Shrine in Norway - 420 miles; walked to Assisi, St. Gilles du Gard, the Cathar Ways and to Mont St. Michel. He has walked every long distance path in France and Germany, and walked to every pilgrimage destination in England and France, and extensively walked in every country in Europe.

He has walked in Africa; all the trails in the Hong Kong Islands; and completed five trekking expeditions to the Himalyas and India. Not only is he the world's leading marathon walker he is Britain's most experienced walker. John is author of more than 440 walk guides which have sold more than 4 million copies with more than 1 million sold on the Peak District. He has created more than 80 challenge walks which have been used to raise, so far, more than a £1 million for different charities.

John has never broken a bone or been lost and never had any trouble anywhere. He still walks in the same body he was born with, has had no replacements and does not use poles. This he puts down to his deep spiritual nature and in 2010 he was ordained as a multi-faith Minister - a universal monk, "honouring and embracing all faiths and none". He conducts weddings and funerals services all over UK and abroad. He teaches Qigong and is a Reiki practioner. He gives illustrated talks on his walks all over the U.K.

CONTENTS

INTRODUCTION

My first book walking and exploring the canals of Derbyshire and Nottinghamshire came out in 1988. Since then, especially on the Chesterfield Canal, there has been major restoration. As a result I decided to rewrite the book and check all the walks out again. At the same time I wanted to expand on what I had done before and this time fully explore each canal end to end. I didn't realise what I had started. Instead of just the one guide I had to split it into three; combined they would be more than double the original!

The Chesterfield Canal, which is somewhat isolated from the rest of the Derbyshire canals, had its own book and went from eight walks to twenty! The Cromford Canal went from just three walks to eleven! This left the remainder of the area with its central hub at Langley Mill. From here the Cromford, Nottingham and Erewash Canals radiate out, with the Nutbrook and Derby Canals branching off the Erewash Canal. Again instead of about fifteen walks on these canals the total has now doubled!

For me it was a never ending joy to retrace some of my steps and see places I first walked twenty years ago. But, with my enquiring mind wanting to explore the missing pieces I walked new paths and came to places and villages I had never visited before. Canal walking is a fascinating pursuit being full of wildlife and history. Some of the canals in this book have been "abandoned", but their history remains and can still be fully seen.

The walks include the River Trent between Trentlock and Nottingham and the Trent & Mersey Canal between Swarkestone, where the Derby Canal joins, to Swarkestone. Together with the River Trent from Shardlow to Trentlock. There are many inns beside the canals; many you can watch the narrow boats pass by. Others you can sit on the banks of the river or canal and soon have a few hungry ducks and swans vying for a piece of bread.

These canal walks, even through the centre of Nottingham, take you into quiet and timeless scenery, where the pace of life is three miles an hour. Put your sandwiches and flask into your pack, winter or summer, and set off along the towpath and let the beauty and history unfold.

ABOUT THE WALKS
- some general comments.

Whilst every care is taken detailing and describing the walks in this book, it should be borne in mind that the countryside changes by the seasons and the work of man. I have described the walk to the best of my ability, detailing what I have found actually on the walk in the way of stiles and signs. Obviously with the passage of time stiles become broken or replaced by a ladder stile , a small gate or a kissing gate. Signs too have a habit of being broken or pushed over - vandelism. All the route follow rights of way and only on rare occasions will you have to overcome obstacles in its path, such as a blown down tree, barbed wire fence or an electric fence. On rare occasions rights of way are rerouted and these ammendments are included in the next edition. Inns have a frustrating habit of changing their name, then back to the original one!

All rights of way have colour coded arrows; on marker posts, stiles/gates and trees; these help you to show the direction of the right of way -

Yellow - Public footpath.
Blue - Public bridleway.
Red - Byway open to all traffic (BOAT).
Black - Road used as a public path (RUPP).

The seasons bring occasional problems whilst out walking which should also be borne in mind. In the height of summer paths become overgrown and you may have to fight your way through in a few places. In low lying areas the fields are often full of crops, and although the pathline goes straight across it may be more practical to walk round the field edge to get to the next stile or gate. In summer the ground is generally dry but in autumn and winter, especially because of our climate, the surface can be decidedly wet and slippery; sometimes even gluttonous mud!

These comments are part of countryside walking which help to make your walk more interesting or briefly frustrating. Standing in a track up to your ankles in mud might not be funny at the time but upon reflection was one of the highlights of the walk!

The mileage for each section is based on three calculations -

1. pedometer reading.
2. the route map measured on the map.
3. the time I took for the walk.

I believe the figure stated for each section to be very accurate but we all walk differently and not always in a straight line! The time allowed for each section is on the generous side and does not include pub stops etc. The figure is based on the fact that on average a person walks 2 1/2 miles an hours but less in hilly terrain. Allow 20 minutes to walk a mile; ten minutes for 1/2 mile and five minutes for 1/4 mile. On average you will walk 2,000 strides to a mile - an average stride is 31 inches..

"For every mile you walk, you extend your life by 21 minutes"

THE CANAL ENGINEERS -

JESSOP AND OUTRAM - These two canal engineers followed on the traditions and work of James Brindley, who surveyed the Chesterfield Canal. These two were partners and based at the famous Butterley Company and their skills complimented each others work. Jessop was the surveyor and builder of canals, while Outram made the tramways and feeder canals.

WILLIAM JESSOP - Born at Davenport in 1745. His first Derbyshire canal was the Cromford Canal. Next was the Nottingham Canal. He is regarded as being the most important engineer of his period and was involved in more canals than anyone. In Codnor Park can be seen the Jessop Monument.

BENJAMIN OUTRAM - Born in Alfreton in 1764. He surveyed the Derby canal, which was adopted and Jessop had a side branch to Little Eaton to link up with a tramway. He was also involved in the Nutbrook Canal and Peak Forest canal from Whaley Bridge, in northern Derbyshire.

JOHN VARLEY - The engineer of the Chesterfield Canal was also involved in the Erewash Canal.

The Great Northern Basin, Langley Mill.

NOTTINGHAM, EREWASH, NUTBROOK, DERBY AND BEESTON CANALS AND THE RIVER TRENT.

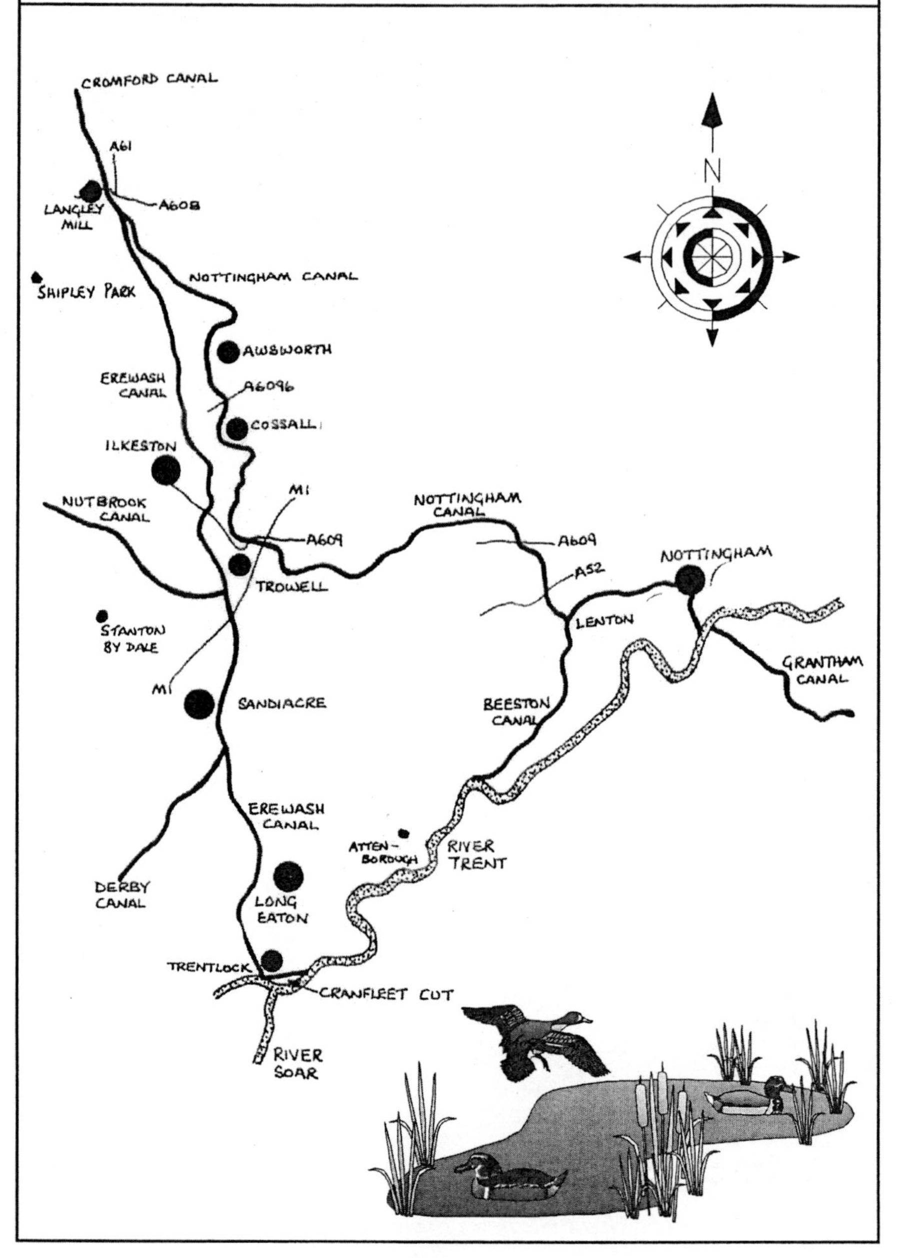

NOTTINGHAM CANAL - HISTORY NOTES

Authorised in 1792. Engineer, William Jessop. Opened in 1796 at a cost of £80,000.

The canal was 14 3/8 miles long from Langley Mill to the River Trent in Nottingham, near Trent Bridge. There were seven short side branches of which the Robbinetts branch is one, near Cossall. There were 20 locks including a flight of 14 at Wollaton. Over the B6007 road near Cossall was a single arch aqueduct; today the canal flows through two large pipes. The canal connected to the Beeston Canal at Lenton Chain.

In 1808 - 269,456 tons of coal was carried on the Cromford, Erewash and Nottingham Canals. The tonnage increased annually until the railways took over, thirty years later.

In 1835 the canal was bought by the Ambergate Railway Company. The section from Langley Mill to Lenton Chain ceased to carry any traffic in 1928 and was abandoned nine years later in 1937. Today, sections of the canal, between Langley Mill and Stapleford are water filled, but the Wollaton part has gone. The section from Lenton Chain to Nottingham and onto the River Trent, together with the Beeston Canal, is still in use today, and a vital link around the River Trent. At Lenton can be seen, on the opposite bank, a boundary stone with the inscribed words - *"The boundary of the Nottingham Canal Company's property, 1885."*

Nottingham Canal Company Seal
- Nottingham Public Library
- Local History Dept.

COSSALL - NOTTINGHAM AND EREWASH CANALS - 9 1/2 MILES

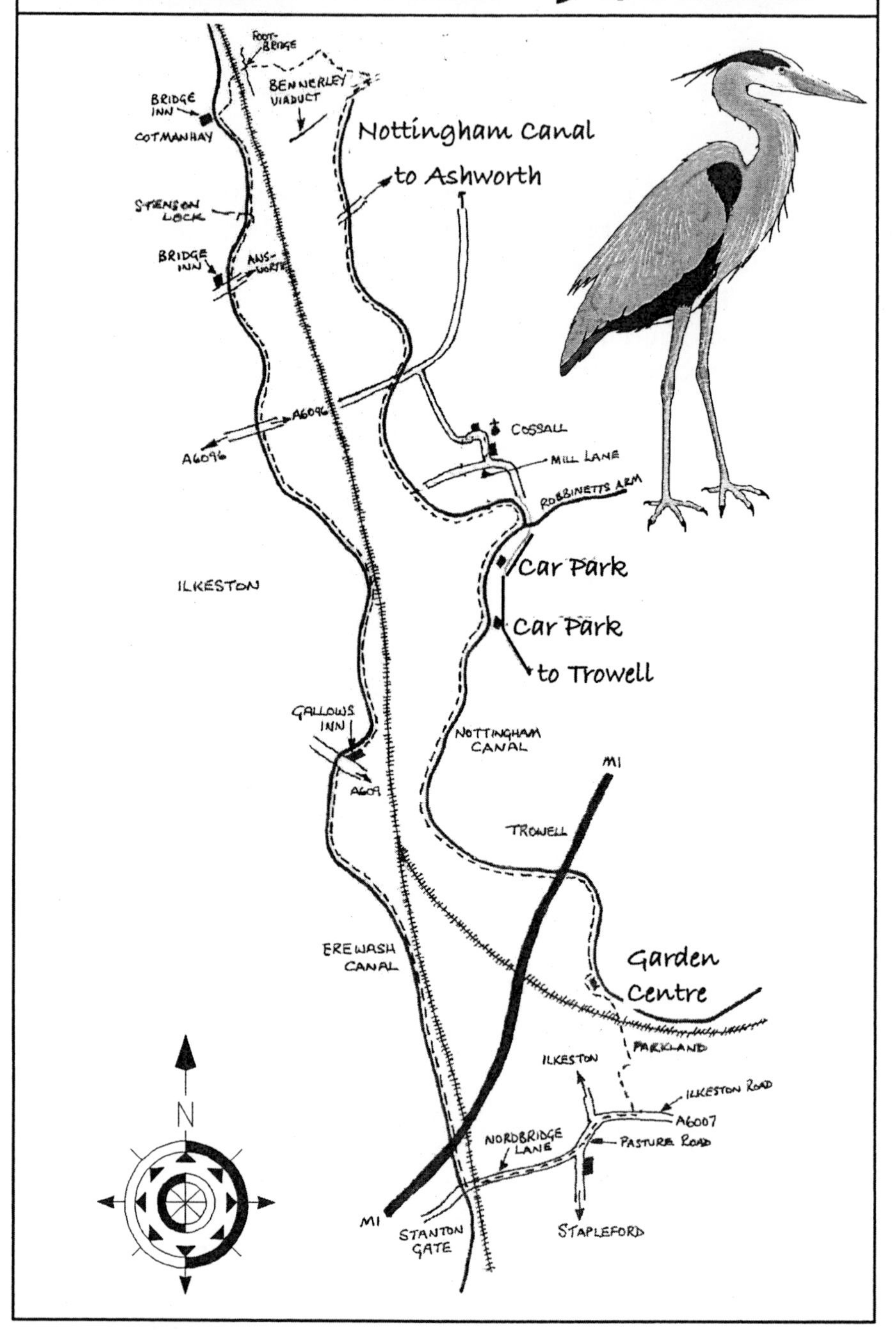

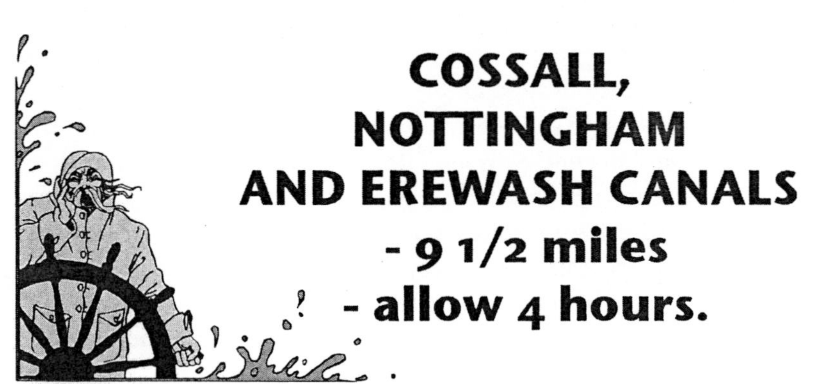

COSSALL, NOTTINGHAM AND EREWASH CANALS - 9 1/2 miles - allow 4 hours.

***Basic route** - Cossall - Nottingham Canal - New Stapleford - Stanton Gate - Erewash Canal - Cotmanhay - Nottingham Canal - Cossall.*

Map - O.S. 1:25,000 Explorer Series No. 260 - Nottingham & the Vale of Belvoir.

Car park and start - Nr. Cossall - lay-by on the Cossall/ Trowell Road with Nottingham Canal Notice Board. Grid Ref. 484415. Alternative beside the road at Grid Ref. 483412; actually on the line of the Nottingham canal.

Inns - Gallows Inn, and two Bridge Inn's, beside the Erewash Canal.

ABOUT THE WALK - You follow almost all that is walkable of the Nottingham Canal before Wollaton, using the Erewash Canal as the linking path. The contrast between a restored and navigable canal with the Nottingham canal now derelict is an interesting comparison. A short road walk through New Stapleford links the two canals at the southern end. The northern link is mostly along paths across the fields, There are several inns enroute beside the Erewash Canal.

WALKING INSTRUCTIONS - Cross the Nottingham Canal and turn left and walk along the towpath with the canal line on your immediate left. Follow the canal for the next 2 miles. After a mile pass houses on your right. Continue and pass under the A609 road and under the M1 bridge. Continue with the canal on your left to Swansea Bridge, which still has the wooden stop gates in position. Beyond is a large garden centre. Turn right just before the bridge and ascend to its right. Turn right and soon left through a kissing gate - Stapleford 1 3/4 m - to walk around the field edge to the garden centre drive. Cross the road and keep ahead, as path signed, on a fenced path with the garden centre on your left. Soon regain the line of the canal on your left. Keep beside it for 200 yards and turn right along a path over the railway line to parkland. Keep straight ahead across the grass and descend to a stile in the far lefthand corner. Turn right then left at the next stile and footbridge. Cross the field on the defined path to the A6007, Ilkeston Road at New Stapleford. Turn right and at the road junction, left along Pasture Road. Take the second road on your right - Morebrige Lane - and follow this to Stanton Gate and the Erewash Canal, 1/2 mile away.

Turn right and walk beside the Erewash Canal on your left. Keep beside the canal for the next 41/2 miles to the Bridge Inn at Cotmanhay. First you pass Junction Lock, the start of the Nutbrook Canal, which is now mostly filled in; it also forms part of the Nutbrook Trail - 9 miles from Shipley Park to Long Eaton - see separate walk. In another mile on the outskirts of Ilkeston you reach the Gallows Inn and lock. Just over two miles later you gain your first Bridge Inn, on your left. Pass Stensons Lock and soon afterwards you pass the impressive Bennerley Viaduct built in 1878; now a Grade 2 listed building, on your right. Just after and before the second Bridge Inn, turn right along a track which soon swings left passing under the railway line. Beyond cross a footbridge over the River Erewash and 100 yards later turn right, as path signed, and follow the distinct path close to the field boundary on your right. Cross a stream and turn left along a good path in trees. In 1/4 mile reach a concrete road on your right. Cross to your right to a fenced path and follow this. It soon swings left to the water filled Nottingham Canal. Turn right and keep the canal on your left for the next 2 1/2 miles.

Crossing the Awsworth road, then the A6096 road, and another road bridge, with the canal water in a pipe, and cross the road at Cossall Marsh. Continue beside the canal on your left for another mile, passing Cossall village to your left and around the loop to the junction of the Robbinetts Arm on your left. 1/4 mile later regain your car park and start.

Nottingham Canal Bridge and stop gates, before Garden Centre.

Bridge Inn, Erewash Canal.

COSSALL, NOTTINGHAM AND EREWASH CANALS - 3 MILES

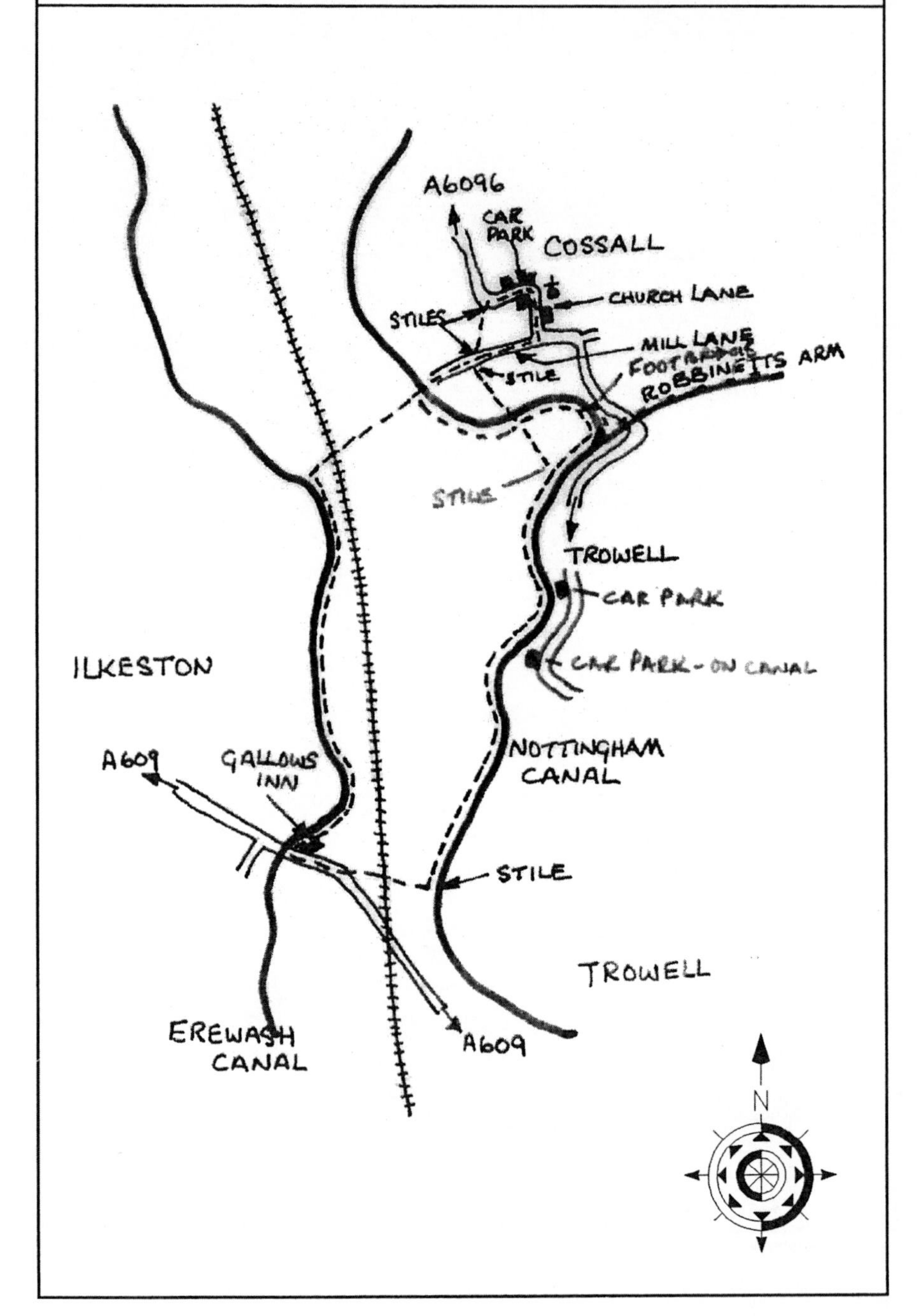

COSSALL, NOTTINGHAM AND EREWASH CANALS - 3 MILES - allow 1 1/2 hours.

Basic Route - Cossall - Nottingham Canal - Gallows Inn - Erewash Canal - Cossall.
The walk can be extended by a mile to explore Cossall and the Robbinetts Arm.

Map - O.S. - 1:25,000 Explorer Series No. 260 - Nottingham & Vale of Belvoir.

Car park and start - Lay by on Cossall/Trowell Road with Nottingham Canal Notice Board. Grid Ref. 484415. Alternative beside the road at Grid Ref. 483412; actually on the Nottingham Canal line.

Inn - Gallows Inn on the Erewash Canal, beside the A6007 road.

ABOUT THE WALK - A short walk linking together the Nottingham and Erewash canals; seeing a preserved one and an abandoned one The village of Cossall is very attractive and full of history with links with D. H. Lawrence and is well worth exploring. You can also explore the short Robbinetts Arm.

WALKING INSTRUCTIONS - Cross the canal, from the car park, and turn left along the Nottingham Canal. In 1/4 mile pass the lower car park on your left. Keep along the tow path for the next 1/2 mile. Where the canal begins to turn left, turn right, as footpath signed, and descend steps past a garden and house on your left, and follow the fenced path to a footbridge over the railway. Continue to the A6007 road. Turn right and follow the road over the Erewash River (the Derbyshire/Nottinghamshire boundary) and gain the Erewash Canal moments later at Gallows Inn. The present inn dates from 1936 and replaces an earlier inn dated 1798; as the name suggests there was a gallows nearby.

Turn right along the towpath with the canal on your left. Follow the canal for a mile and just before the Ilkeston Lock - (second lock) - turn right along the path, first over a footbridge over the Erewash River, then across the railway line, before continuing up a track to the Nottingham Canal. 1/4 mile away.

If you want explore Cossall, cross the canal here and continue on the track, now Mill Lane to the road on the southern side of Cossall. Turn left to see the church, Church Cottage and the Willoughby Almshouses. Return the same way back to the canal.

Turn right along the canal which soon does a loop contouring round the level to the junction of the Robbinetts Arm on your left. Before the junction there is a footbridge on your left and by crossing this and turning right along the other side of the canal you can explore this arm to the Cossall/Trowell Road. Cross over and see some more of the visible remains of the arm; return the same way back to the junction. Continue on the towpath for little over 1/4 mile back to the car park.

COSSALL - The Church dedicated to St. Catherine dates from the 12th century. Close to the gate is the Waterloo Memorial, 1877, recording three locals who took part in the famous battle. Church Cottage was the home of D. H. Lawrence's fiancé and is featured in his novel - The Rainbow; The Willoughby Almshouses were built by George Willoughby in 1685. The family built Wollaton Hall.

Bennerley Viaduct.

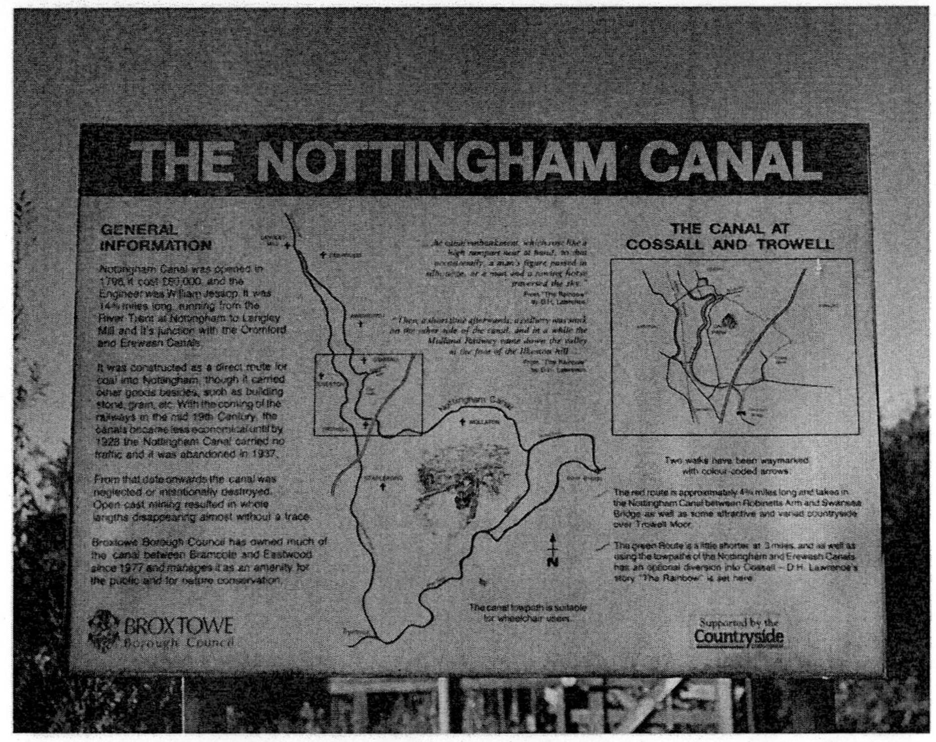

Nottingham Canal Notice Board at Canal Car Park.

Nottingham Canal, near Cossall.

NOTTINGHAM CANAL - BRAMCOTE AND STAPLEFORD HILLS - 4 MILES

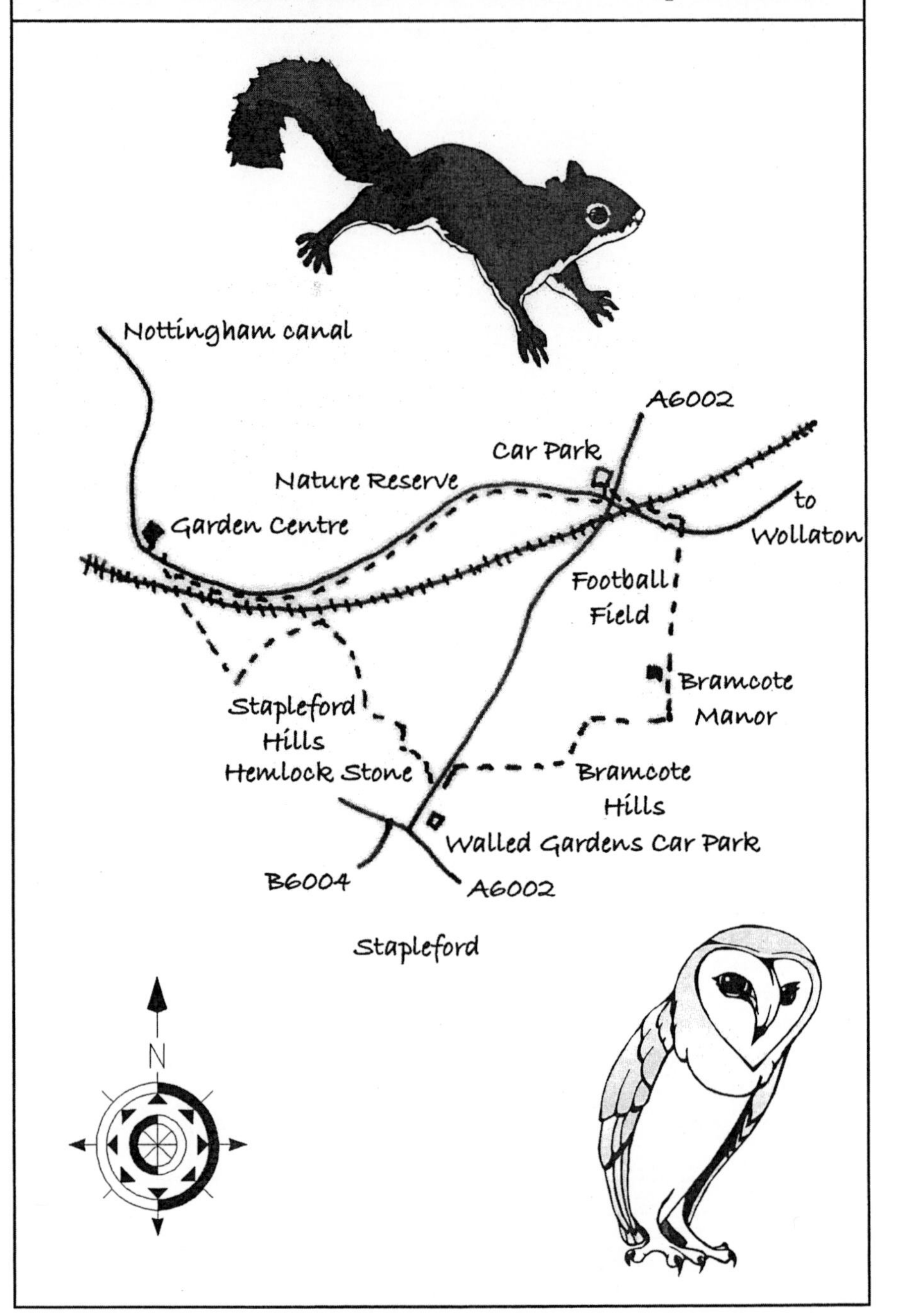

NOTTINGHAM CANAL, BRAMCOTE AND STAPLEFORD HILLS - 4 MILES - allow 1 1/2 hours.

Basic Route - A6002 - Nottingham canal - Bramcote Hill -Hemlock Stone - Stapleford Hill - Nottingham canal - A6002.

Map - O.S. 1:25,000 Explorer Series No. 260 - Nottingham.

Car Park and start - just off the A6002 - Nottingham Canal and local Nature Reserve car park. Grid Ref. 505395. Alternative - the Walled Gardens Car Park, on the A6002, opposite the Hemlock Stone.

Inn - Bramcote Manor, before the Bramcote Hill.

ABOUT THE WALK - A short walk along the last section of the Nottingham Canal before the outskirts of Nottingham and Wollaton Park. You join the Robin Hood's Way and ascend Bramcote and Stapleford Hills, with views before gaining the disused canal and following back to the A6002.

WALKING INSTRUCTIONS - From the car park ascend back to the road and cross it as path signed. Follow the path in woodland close to the line of the Nottingham canal. In less than 1/4 mile nearing houses, turn right along a tarred path, with a large football field on your right. Follow the path straight ahead for more than 1/4 mile and pass the

Bramcote Manor Inn to your right. A few yards later beside House No. 15, turn right onto a fenced path, now on the Robin Hood's Way. The path is tarmaced and is signed Bramcote Hill. Soon turn left and ascend passing a school on your left, and bear right later high on the hill and follow the wide path down and right to steps and onto the A6002 road near the Walled Garden car park - to your left. At the A6002, turn left and in a few yards right and ascend to the Hemlock Stone and Information board. Continue on the path behind and continue ascending to the summit of Stapleford Hill and trig point. Continue straight ahead down the other side, ignoring turnings and at the bottom leave the woodland and walk along the lefthand side of a field. Follow it to the second stile on your left. Over, in a few yards ascend the steps to a level grass area. Turn left keeping to the righthand side and reach the path on your right. Turn right and cross a railway bridge and gain the Nottingham canal. Turn right along the towpath and follow the canal for almost a mile back to the car park and start.

Nottingham Canal bridge before regaining the car park.

HEMLOCK STONE - The solitary stone has long been popular with the Druids and Celtic customs and many legends are woven about the mysteries of the stone. In more recent times, on the occasion of King George III Golden Jubilee on October 25th. 1809, a bullock was roasted on the top and used to feed the locals of Stapleford. On the occasion of Elizabeth II Golden Jubilee, a beacon was lit on the summit.

NOTTINGHAM CANAL IN NOTTINGHAM - 3 MILES

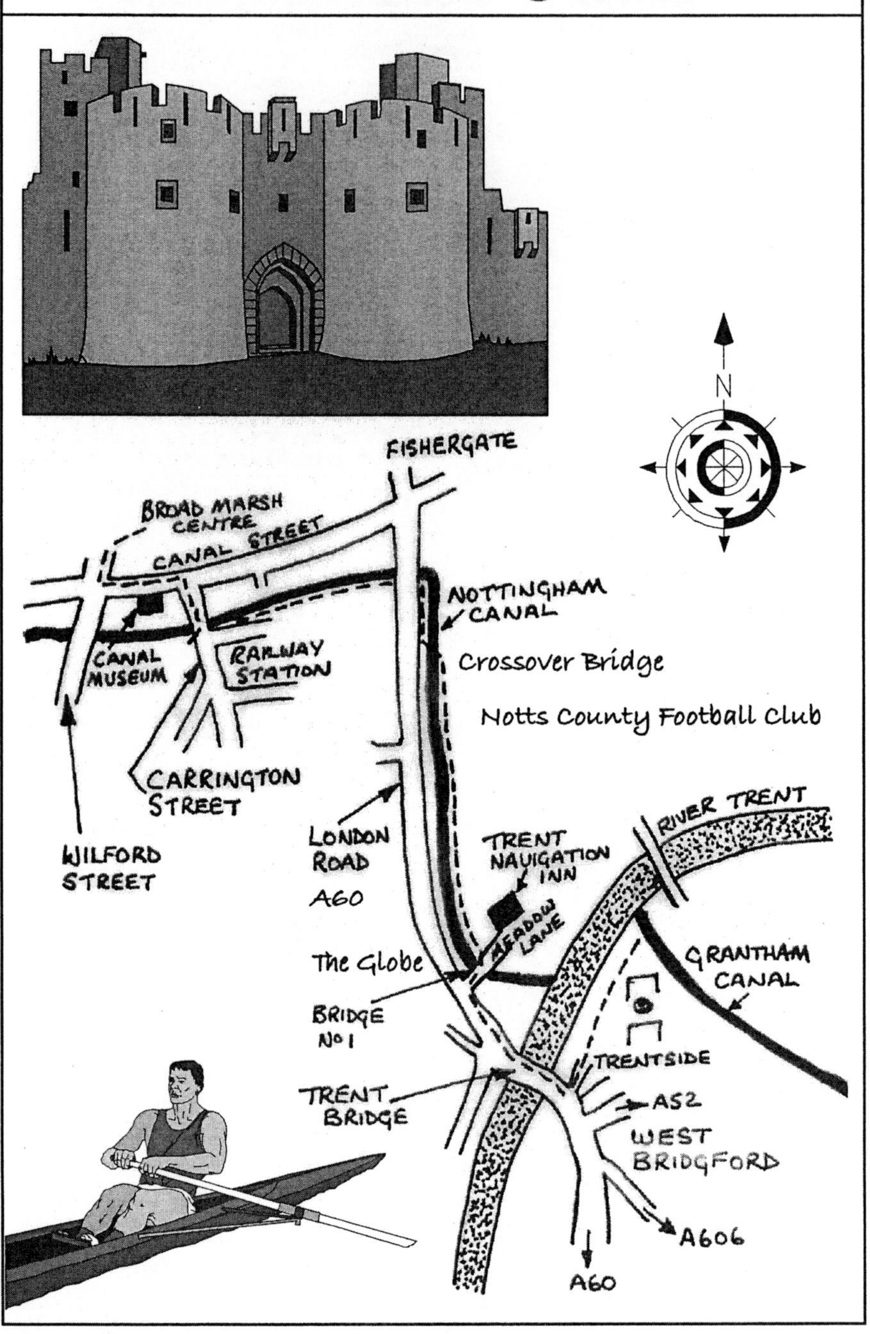

NOTTINGHAM CANAL IN NOTTINGHAM - 3 MILES - allow 1 1/2 hours

Basic Route - Broad Marsh Centre - Canal Street - Carrington Street - Nottingham Canal - Trent Bridge - Start of Grantham Canal - Nottingham Canal - Broad Marsh Centre.

Map - O.S. 1:25,000 Explorer Series No. 260 - Nottingham.

Car park and start - Broad Marsh Centre, Nottingham,

Inns - Navigation Inn, Castle Lock; just off the route near start. Canal House Bar & Restaurant, off Canal Street. Hooter's Bar & Restaurant, just off the canal. Trent Navigation Inn and the Globe Inn, at the end of the canal section. Casa Bar & Restaurant before Trent Bridge. The Southbank Bar, north side of Trent Bridge.

ABOUT THE WALK - A city walk but one along the quiet haven of the canal to the River Trent. In many ways this is an ideal family walk to familiarise yourself with canal walking. Gaining the canal you follow it to near the River Trent. Here close to the Trent Navigation Inn, as you cannot continue to the Trent Lock, you gain the road and cross Trent Bridge. Just past the Nottingham Forest Football stadium you see the start of the Nottingham Canal, opposite across the river. A short distance ahead is the lock and start of the Grantham Canal. A canal that is fully explored in the Nottinghamshire and Lincolnshire Canal walk book in this series. You can also start the walk from the Broad Marsh Bus Station.

WALKING INSTRUCTIONS - Exit the southern end of the car park or bus station into Canal Street. Turn left then right along Carrington Street and in a few yards right to gain the Nottingham Canal towpath. To your left is the impressive British Waterways Board warehouse. Turn right and walk along the towpath with the canal on your left and pass under London Road and follow the canal sharp right to a crossover bridge. Cross and continue now with the canal on your right. Follow it past the Notts County Football ground. A further 1/2 mile with The Globe Inn to your right, leave the canal on your left and cross a bridge - to your left is the Trent Navigation Inn - and gain London Road. (You can continue a little further along the towpath to the fencing before the lock to the River Trent.) Turn left along the road and cross Trent Bridge. At the otherside turn left to walk along the banks of the river, on a tarmaced road, past the Nottingham Forest Football Ground and the Brian Clough Stadium. On your left across the river can be see where the Nottingham Canal enters the River Trent. Continue ahead a little further, now on a path to the lock and start of the Grantham Canal. Retrace your steps back to Canal Street and the Broad Marsh Centre.

Nottingham Canal in Central Nottingham.

Crossover Bridge; Nottingham Canal.

The River Trent with the entrance lock to the Nottingham Canal.

BEESTON CANAL

Built in 1795 and 2 1/2 miles long from the River Trent to Lenton Chain, where it joined the Nottingham Canal. The River Trent was difficult to pass through at the Wilford Shoals near West Bridgford, and this short canal helped to alleviate the problem. The name Lenton Chain derives from the Trent Navigation Company. From Saturday evening to Monday morning they used to lock the canal by placing a chain across it; Grid Ref. 554386.

The start of the Beeston Canal, from the River Trent.

Beeston Canal Lock, at start of the canal.

The Beeston Canal beyond the lock.

ATTENBOROUGH, RIVER TRENT & BEESTON CANAL - 4 1/2 MILES

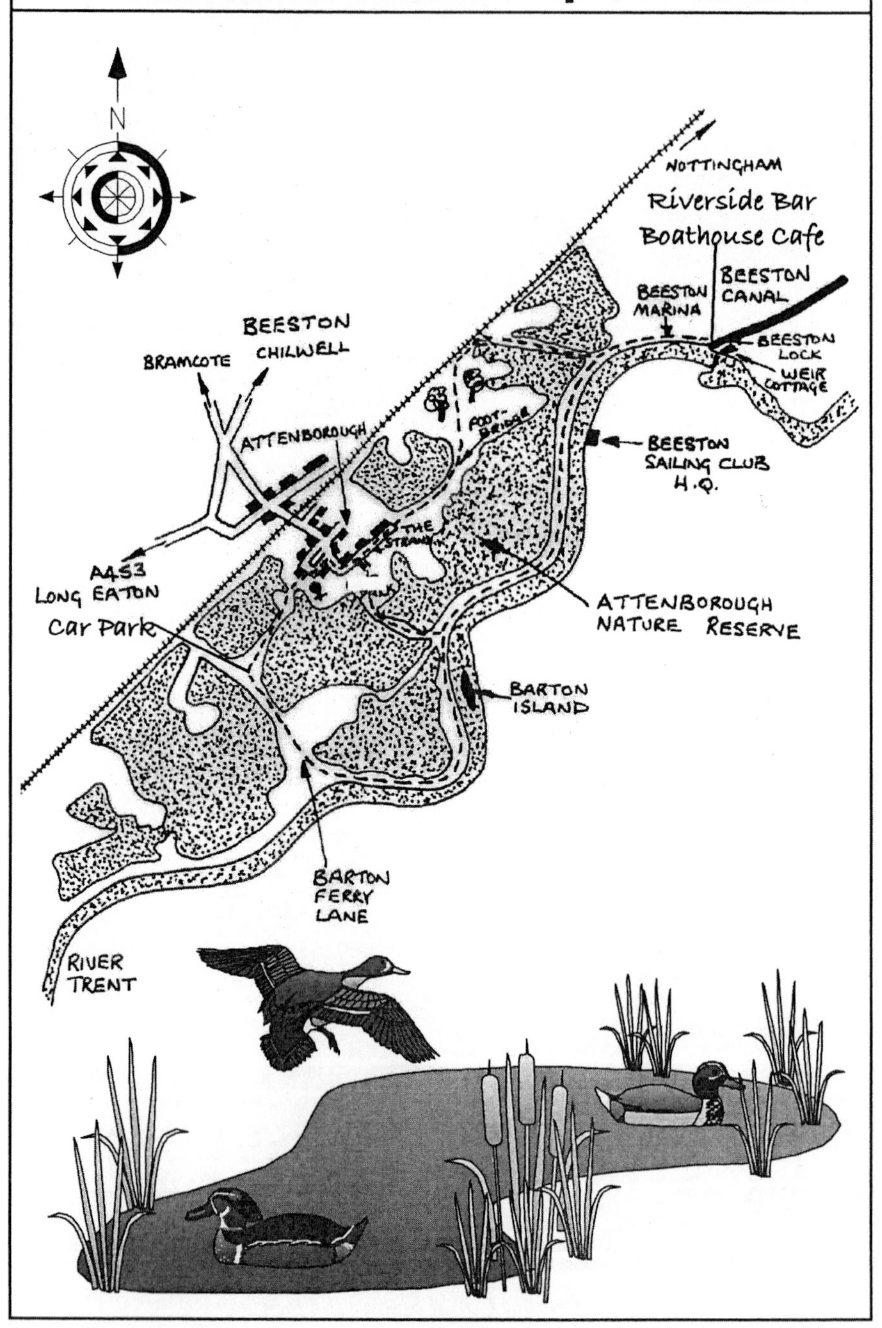

ATTENBOROUGH, RIVER TRENT & BEESTON CANAL - 4 1/2 MILES - allow 2 hours.

Basic Route** - **Barton Lane Car Park** - **River Trent** - **Attenborough Nature Reserve** - **Beeston Marina** - **Beeston Lock** - **Attenborough Nature Reserve** - **Attenborough** - **Barton Lane Car Park.

Map** - **O.S. 1:25,000 Explorer Series No. 260** - **Nottingham.

Car Park and start** - **Barton Lane Carpark off the A6005 road. Grid Ref. 516339.

Inn** - **Riverside Bar, Beeston Marina.

Teas** - **Boathouse Cafe, Beeston Marina.

ABOUT THE WALK - At the beginning and end of the walk you walk through the Attenborough Nature Reserve - old gravel pits - where an amazing variety of birds have been spotted - more than 200 different species. It is a good place to carry your binoculars. Next you walk beside the navigable River Trent, which links Trentlock with Beeston Lock; here is an inn and tea-room. You can extend the walk by walking the Beeston Canal and Lock 3 mile walk. After exploring the start of the canal you return via the former gravel pits back to Attenborough and St. Mary the Virgin church, before regaining the car park.

WALKING INSTRUCTIONS - From the car park turn left and cross the bridge over a channel and continue straight ahead along the track/ path (bridlepath) to the River Trent less than 1/2 mile away. Turn left and walk along the banks of the river for the next two miles - Riverside path to Beeston & Nottingham, passing two signed paths to your left. The second one, signed "Meadow Lane", is the path you will take after visiting Beeston Lock. Keep ahead past the boats of Beeston Marina and in 1/4 mile pass the Riverside Bar and Boathouse Tea-room before gaining the Beeston Canal and Lock.

Retrace your steps back more than 1/4 mile to the path sign - "Meadow Lane". Turn right and follow the path to near the railway line, more than 1/4 mile away. Before it, as signed, turn left for Attenborough Village. After keeping near the railway line the path bears left then right over a bridge over the gravel pits, as you regain the Attenborough Nature Reserve. Gaining the road in the village keep straight ahead along it and follow it right before turning left along Church Lane, to pass St. Mary the Virgin church on your left; its tall spire is a landmark throughout the walk. Just past the church turn left, as path signed, along the drive of Ireton House, pass the stables on your left and follow the path/track over a bridge between the lakes and regain the car park.

ATTENBOROUGH GRAVEL PITS - A Nature Reserve mostly of reed beds and open water and is a popular bird watching area, with over 217 species recorded. Many migratory birds pass through including spoonbill and little crake. Waterfowl are predominant and all year round can be seen, reed bunting, tufted duck, pochard, teal, grebe, shoveler, great crested grebe, little grebe, mallard, moorhens, snipe and numerous gulls.

Beeston Marina and River Trent.

ST. MARY THE VIRGIN CHURCH, ATTENBOROUGH - Dates from the 12th. century and inside the porch can be seen old grave slabs. The spire was built in the 14th. century. Oliver Cromwell stabled his horses in the nave. The adjacent Ireton House includes parts of the earlier house. Here two brothers were born; John Ireton, born 1615, who became Lord Mayor of London and Henry Ireton, born 1611, married Cromwell's daughter, Bridget.

BEESTON CANAL AND LOCK - 3 MILES

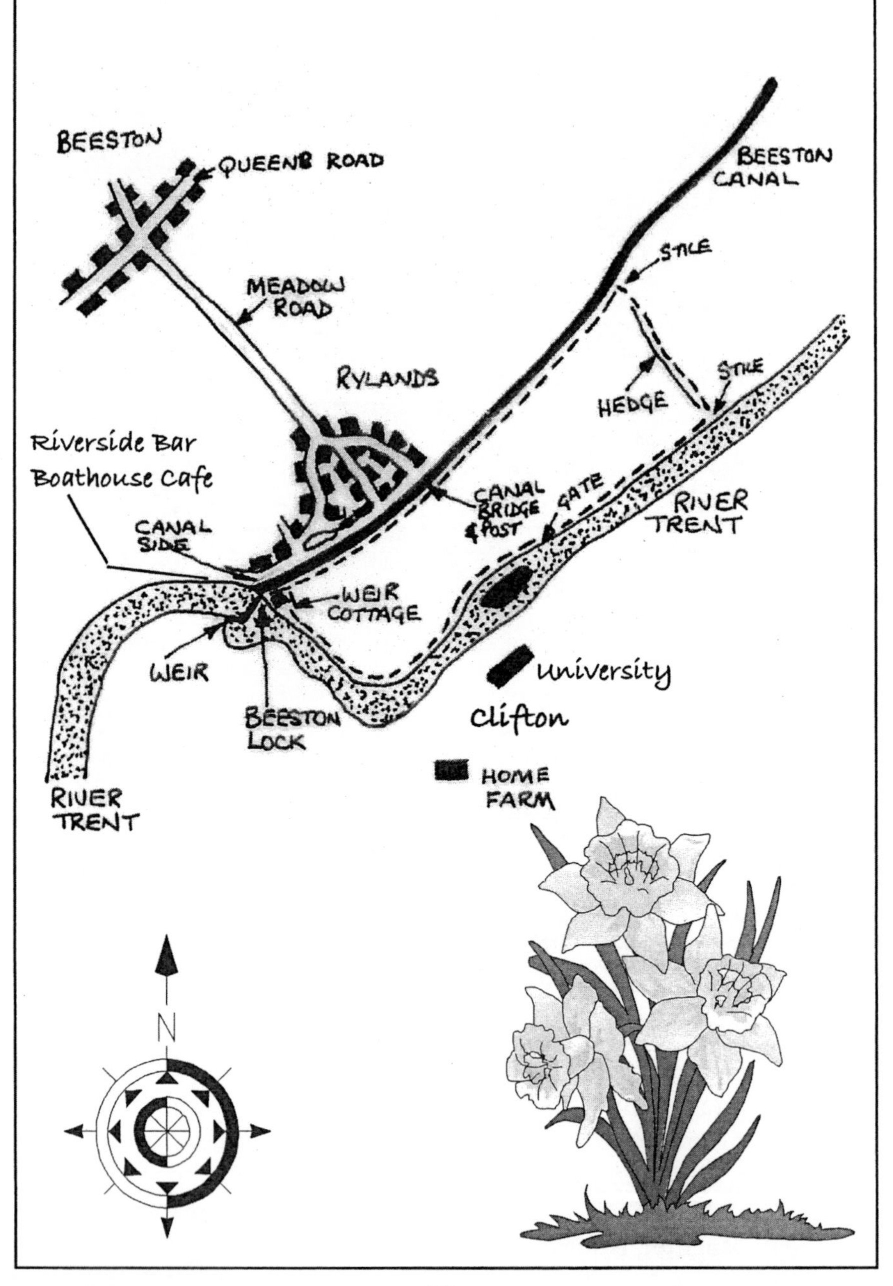

BEESTON CANAL AND LOCK - 3 MILES - allow 1 1/2 hours.

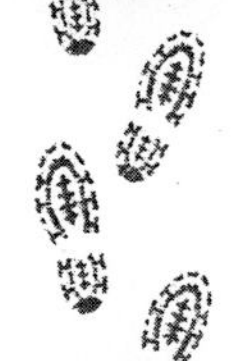

Basic route - Beeston Lock - River Trent - Beeston Canal - Beeston Lock.

Map - O.S. 1:25,000 Explorer Series No. 260 - Nottingham

Car park and start - Roadside parking on Canal Side Road, Rylands, near Beeston Lock. Grid Ref. 536354.

Inn - Riverside Bar, Beeston Marina.

Teas - Boathouse Cafe, Beeston Marina.

ABOUT THE WALK - A short circular walk around the early part of the canal, first beside the River Trent to see the impressive weir before passing the wooded slops of Clifton on the otherside of the river. After 1 1/2 mile you cross a field to gain the Beeston canal and follow it back to its lock and your start. The walk can be added to the Attenborough walk, making a rewarding 7 mile route.

WALKING INSTRUCTIONS - Cross Beeston Lock via a footbridge, with Weir Cottage on the right. Cross a subsequent bridge and turn right

- the route ahead, along the canal, is your return path. The path leads to the banks of the River Trent, and a side path to your right brings you to a vantage point over the weir. Follow the defined path along the banks of the river, as it turns left with the wooded slopes of Clifton on the otherside. Keep beside the river for almost another mile (18 minutes), passing Cherry Island at the midway point. Pass a rugby field on your left and well before the next one, turn left at a path sign, and follow the defined path beside the hedge on your left to a track. *(A pipe overflow into the River Trent is the turning point.)* Turn left to a stile and immediately right to steps over the wall and gain the canal towpath. Turn left beside the canal. At the first canal bridge gain the path above the canal and follow it back to Beeston Lock. The inn and tea-room are just a little further beside the River Trent.

The River Trent Weir near Beeston Marina.

A narrowboat, looking somewhat out of place on the River Trent.

The Beeston Canal.

BEESTON & NOTTINGHAM CANAL - 4 1/2 MILES

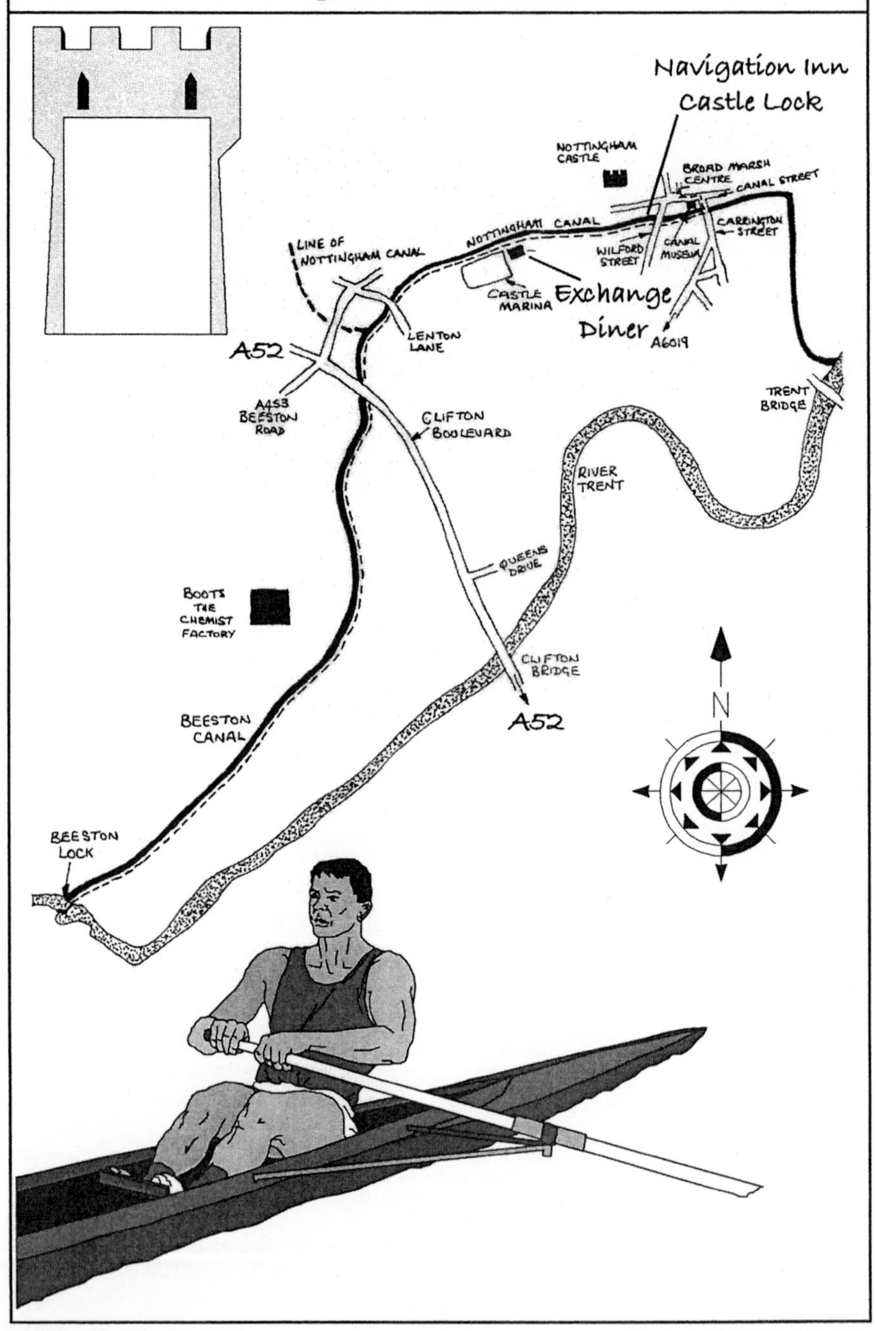

BEESTON AND NOTTINGHAM CANAL - 4 1/2 MILES - allow 2 hours (Round trip 9 miles - allow 4 hours.)

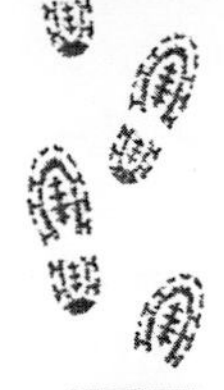

***Basic Route** - Beeston Lock - Beeston Canal - Lenton - Nottingham Canal - Castle Marina - Castle Lock - Carrington Street - Broad Marsh Centre. You can start from the Broadmarsh Centre and walk to Beeston Lock and the River Trent and return the same way (9 miles).*

***Map** - O.S. 1:25,000 Explorer Series No. 260 - Nottingham.*

***Car Park and start** - Canal Side at Beeston Lock or the Broad Marsh Centre.*

***Inns** - Riverside Bar, Beeston marina. Exchange Diner, near Castle Marina. Navigation Inn, Castle Lock. Canalhouse Bar and Restaurant, close to Carrington Street and Canal Street, Nottingham.*

***Teas** - Boathouse Tea Room, Beeston Marina.*

ABOUT THE WALK - A very pleasant walk from the River Trent to central Nottingham, along the whole length of the Beeston Canal to its "lost" junction with the Nottingham Canal. You can either do it as a one-way walk or return the same way, walking from either Beeston Lock or from the Broad Marsh Centre. I fully recommend the latter for it is surprising how different everything looks from the opposite direction!

WALKING INSTRUCTIONS - Starting from Beeston Lock - round to your right is Beeston Marina with bar and tea room - cross the footbridge and turn left along the towpath above the canal. On your right is Weir Fields Recreation area. Pass a bridge on your left to Canal Side and gain the towpath beside the Beeston Canal on your left. In more than a mile pass under the Boots road bridge with their factory to your left. Continue on the canal towpath and in another mile pass under another bridge as you get closer to the central part of Nottingham. Pass under another bridge and soon afterwards a railway bridge and then A52 bridge. Pass an interesting collection of memorabilia beside the canal on your left, close to the "lost" junction of the Nottingham canal, at Lenton Chain. Continue now beside the Nottingham Canal, passing the Trevethick Boat Builders yard on your left. Pass under Lenton Street and 1/4 mile later another railway line. Just after on your left in the wall can be seen the Nottingham Canal Company's Property boundary stone, dated 1885. Pass Castle Marina on your right with views to Nottingham Castle. Continue beside the canal over a footbridge with Exchange Diner on your right. Soon on your right is Tinkers Leen which runs to the River Trent and was an industrial water source. Pass the Inland Revenue offices on your right before the Castle Lock and Navigation Inn on your left. Pass the Magistrates Court on your right and on your left the British Waterways Board warehouse and the canal haulage company - Fellows, Morton and Clayton Ltd. Just after is the Canalhouse Bar and Restaurant on your left. Leave the canal her and gain Carrington Street. Turn left to Canal Street and left then right to the Broad Marsh car park and bus station.

Trevethick Boat Builders.

Nottingham Canal near Castle Marina with view to Nottingham astle.

Castle Lock.

BEESTON CANAL, NOTTINGHAM CANAL AND THE RIVER TRENT - 14 MILES

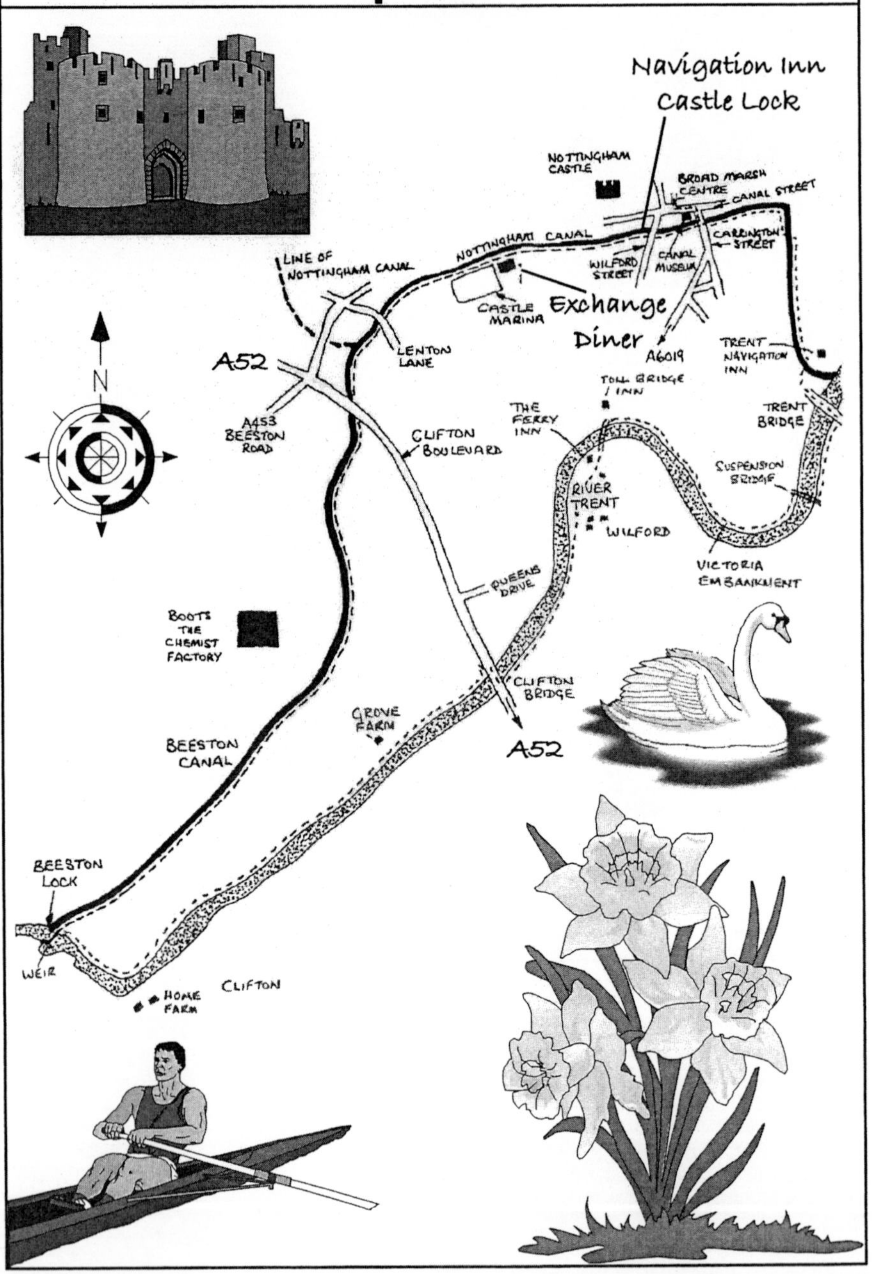

BEESTON CANAL, NOTTINGHAM CANAL AND RIVER TRENT - 14 MILES - allow 5 hours

***Basic Route** - Beeston Lock - Beeston Canal - Lenton - Nottingham Canal - Castle Marina - Castle Lock - Trent Navigation Inn - Trent Bridge - Start of Grantham Canal - River Trent - Suspension Bridge - Victoria Embankment - Wilford Toll Bridge - Wilford - River Trent - Clifton Bridge - River Trent - Trent Valley Way - Beeston Lock.*

***Map** - O.S. 1:25,000 Explorer Series No. 260 - Nottingham.*

***Car Park and start** - Canal Side at Beeston Lock or the Broad Marsh Centre.*

***Inns** - Riverside Bar, Beeston Marina. Exchange Diner, near Castle Marina. Navigation Inn, Castle Lock. Canalhouse Bar and Restaurant, close to Carrington Street and Canal Street, Nottingham. Trent Navigation Inn, the Globe Inn, Casa Bar & Restaurant, and Southbank Bar near Trent Bridge. Toll Bridge Inn, near Wilford Toll Bridge. The Ferry Inn, Wilford.*

***Teas** - Boathouse Tea Room, Beeston Marina.*

ABOUT THE WALK - A magnificent walk along the Beeston Canal and Nottingham Canal through central Nottingham to the River Trent.

Here a side trip brings you opposite the point where the Nottingham Canal begins and the start of the Grantham Canal. From here you basically follow the River Trent south westerly to Wilford and after crossing the Clifton Bridge, walk along its banks back to Beeston Lock, where you began. A long but level walk full of contrasts in a busy city, following quiet paths.

WALKING INSTRUCTIONS - Starting from Beeston Lock - round to your right is Beeston Marina with bar and tea room - cross the footbridge and turn left along the towpath above the canal. On your right is Weir Fields Recreation area. Pass a bridge on your left to Canal Side and gain the towpath beside the Beeston Canal on your left. In more than a mile pass under the Boots road bridge with their factory to your left. Follow the canal towpath and in another mile pass under another bridge as you get closer to the central part of Nottingham. Pass under another bridge and soon afterwards a railway bridge and then A52 bridge. Pass an interesting collection of memorabilia beside the canal on your left, close to the "lost" junction of the Nottingham canal at Lenton Chain. Continue now beside the Nottingham Canal, passing the Trevethick Boat Builders yard on your left. Pass under Lenton Street and 1/4 mile later a railway line. Just after on your left in the wall can be seen the Nottingham Canal Company's Property boundary stone, dated 1885. Pass Castle Marina on your right with views to Nottingham Castle. Continue beside the canal over a footbridge with Exchange Diner on your right. Soon on your right is Tinkers Leen which runs to the River Trent and was an industrial water source. Pass the Inland Revenue offices on your right before the Castle Lock and Navigation Inn on your left. Pass the Magistrates Court on your right and on your left the British Waterways Board warehouse and the canal haulage company - Fellows, Morton and Clayton Ltd. Just after is the Canalhouse Bar and Restaurant on your left. To your left is Canal Street and the Broad Marsh car park and bus station.

Continue on the towpath and pass under the A60 - London Road. Here the canal turns sharp right and soon reach a crossover bridge. Cross over and continue on the lefthand side of the canal, with the canal now on your right. In 1/2 mile with the Globe Inn on your right and the Trent Navigation Inn on your left, leave the canal cross the canal bridge to the A60 road. Turn left and across Trent Bridge and turn left along the tarmaced surface past rowing clubs to the Notts Forest Football Ground. Across the river can be seen the start of the Nottingham canal. Beyond the ground reach the lock and start of the Grantham Canal. Retrace you steps to Trent Bridge and walk under it to continue on the embankment, past County Hall on your left, to a suspension bridge. Cross and turn left to continue now with the river on your left along Victoria Embankment. During spring the embankment are adorned with swathes of daffodils. Keep beside the river for a mile to the next bridge - Wilford Toll Bridge, which replaced a ferry here, with a monument to Sir Robert Jukes Clifton, Bart MP - 1861 - 69. To your right is the Toll Bridge Inn. Turn left over the now pedestrianised bridge. The toll house displays the tolls, following the Wilford Bridge Act of 1862.

*"For every ass drawing or carrying more than 1 person ....1d.
For every ox, bull or neat cattle 1 penny; or a score ...6d.
Coaches and carriages .....6d.
Mule or horse ......1 1/2d.
Horse and wagon ....4d."*

Continue on the road from the bridge past The Ferry Inn and through Wilford. Regaining the bankside pass St. Wilfrid's church to your right - dates from the 13th. century. Where the road leaves the bankside, keep right as sign posted - River Trent Greenway - Clifton and Barton in Fabis. Follow the path to the road and A52 Clifton Bridge. Walk under the bridge before turning left, crossing the road and ascending steps to the bridge; signed City Centre. Turn left along it and follow the tarmaced path down from the bridge to a junction. Turn left along the lane passing Greenwood Football Club on your right and onto a gate. Beyond turn left to the bridge and then right along the track along its bank. Soon gain a drive and where it turns right to Grove Farm Sports Ground, keep ahead now on a path along the banks of the river. Soon with path signs - Trent Valley Way. Follow the path for over 1 1/2 miles with the woodland of Clifton on the otherside of the river. The river turns right and in more than 1/4 mile reach a weir and just after Weir Cottage and bridge over Beeston Lock and your start. To your left is Beeston Marina.

Nottingham Canal in central Nottingham.

Trent Bridge.

The start of the Gratham Canal, with the Brian Clough Stadium behind.

River Trent Suspension Bridge.

EREWASH CANAL
some brief history notes -

Authorised in 1777, Capital of £23,000 was raised by £100 shares. John Varley, who had been involved with the Chesterfield Canal, was appointed the engineer at a salary of £220 per annum. Pinkerton Brothers were the joint contractors, The canal was opened in July 1779 and had taken only 20 months to dig at a cost of £21,000. The canal - 11 3/4 miles long - ran from Trentlock to Langley Mill, closely following the river Erewash. In its length were 14 locks rising 109 feet from Trentlock to Langley Mill. The locks were wide gauge to take the Upper Trent Wide Boats which were 70 feet long by 14 feet wide.

The relatively cheap cost of the canal plus the abundance of trade from the surrounding area, made the canal one of the most prosperous in Britain. At its height a share was worth £1,300 and in 1826 a dividend of 74% was paid.

The decline was partly due to the coming of the railway, being both cheaper and quicker than canals, but also because of the high tolls charged by the Erewash Canal Company. In an effort to revitalise it this century, the Grand Union Canal Company bought it in 1932, with others, but it was too late, and it was passed to the British Waterways Board upon Nationalisation. By the middle of this century it was little used and in 1962 the section from Gallows Inn in Ilkeston to Langley Mill was classed unnavigable, but was used occasionally. Six years later in 1968, the Transport Act declared the canal closed to navigation from Long Eaton to Langley Mill.

There the canal might have been left to decay and one of the great transport routes on the Midlands might have been lost. But, in 1968 a Canal Preservation Society was formed to save the canal. It has been their single-mindedness that has saved such a historic canal from abandonment. The Great Northern Basin was restored and reopened on May 26th 1973. Almost ten years later in February 1983, the Erewash Canal was upgraded from a 'Remainder' waterway to a 'Cruise way'.

Great Northern Basin and first Erewash Canal lock.

Long Eaton Lock - Erewash Canal.

SHIPLEY PARK, GREAT NORTHERN BASIN AND THE EREWASH CANAL - 7 MILES

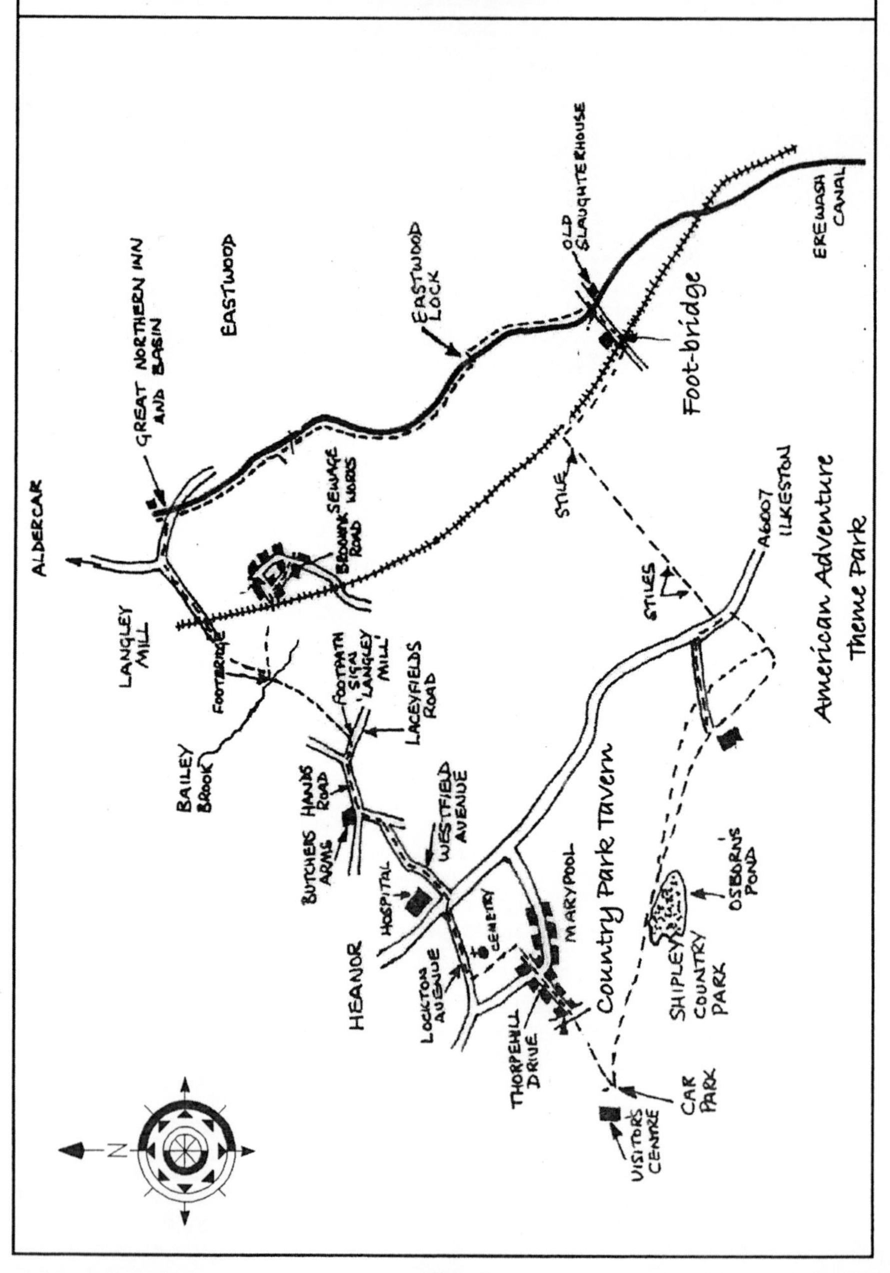

SHIPLEY COUNTRY PARK, GREAT NORTHERN BASIN AND THE EREWASH CANAL - 7 MILES - allow 3 hours.

Basic Route - Shipley Country Park - Marlpool - Langley - Langley Mill - Great Northern Basin - Erewash Canal - Shipley Lock - Bentley's Plantation - A6007 - American Adventure - Shipley Country Park.

Map - O.S. 1:25,000 Explorer Series No. 260 - Nottingham.

Car park and start - Shipley Country Park - Visitor's Centre - Heanor Gate End. Grid Ref. 432454.

Inns - Country Park Tavern, Marlpool. Butcher's Arms, Langley. Erewash Inn, Railway Tavern, The Mill and Great Northern in Langley Mill.

ABOUT THE WALK - The first mile involves passing through the houses of Marlpool and Langley, before following a path to Langley Mill. A short road walk brings you to the Great Northern Basin, where the Erewash, Nottingham and Cromford Canals meet; the latter two are now disused. From the historic basin you follow the Erewash Canal for a couple miles past locks to Shipley Lock. Here you head westwards following a former tramway line that brought coal from Shipley to the canal and onward transport. You pass the American Adventure Theme Park before walking through Shipley Country Park back to the car park near the Visitor's Centre.

WALKING INSTRUCTIONS - Turn left at the top of the car park, by the Information board, and where the path turns right and descends - your return path - keep slightly left to follow a descending path aiming for the lefthand side of the Country Park Tavern. Keep straight ahead past the tavern to a road. Go straight across and continue along Thorpe Hill Drive to the main road. Go straight across onto a tarmaced drive and after 50 yards by no. 69A The Bungalow, turn left onto a tarmaced path with Marlpool Cemetery on your right and passing a new part on your left. In 1/4 mile reach Lockton Avenue and turn right along this to the A6007 road. Turn right then left into Westfield Avenue and soon start descending with views to the canal and basin. Descend and at the bottom bear left to Hands Road and the Butchers Arms. Turn right along Hands Lane and take the second road on your right - Laceyfields Road. In a few yards by house no. 5 turn left onto a tarmaced footpath. Follow this past houses on your left to a footbridge and onto an Industrial Estate road. Cross over to continue on the path, passing Mills Computer Products on your right. Follow this to the A608 road by St. Andrews church on your left. Turn right passing the Erewash Inn on your left. Pass the Langley railway station and continue on past the Railway Tavern and The Mill. Just after cross the River Erewash and turn turn left along Boundary Lane to the Great Northern basin and Erewash Canal.

Turn right along the canal towpath past Langley Mill Lock - the River Trent is 14 3/4 miles' away at TrentLock. Walk beside the canal on your left and a mile later reach Eastwood Lock. Cross over the bridge and continue now with the canal on your right and in 1/2 mile reach Shipley Lock. Gain the road bridge and turn right. Follow the road past the former Shipley Boat Inn to a footbridge over the railway line. Turn right along a road beside the line and in more than 1/4 mile where it turns right, on your left is a stile. Follow the defined path which soon follows, ascending gently, the line of a former tramway. In 1/2 mile go through a stile on your right and continue up the lefthand side of the field to a stile and onto the A6007 road. Go straight across and descend steps and continue along the former railway line, turning left passing a football field on your right, and gain the car park and entrance area of the American Adventure Theme park. Turn right into Shipley Country park, passing Shipley Woodhouse Colliery, which closed in 1960, on your left. The tarmaced "road" is signed for the Visitor's Centre. You can follow this back to Osbornes' Pool or you can turn right in a few yards and follow another former railway line that eventually meets the other route near the pool. Here continue on the main path past the lake on your left and following the track reach large stone posts and open space on your left. Turn left along a path and ascend to the path junction near the car park where you began a few hours ago. The Visitor's Centre is to your left and well worth a visit.

SHIPLEY COUNTRY PARK - Opened in 1975 and includes the remains of Shipley Hall, its gardens and lakes. A quarter of the area was colliery waste heaps and these have been landscaped and Shipley Lake (now part of the American Adventure Theme Park), was reformed. There is a mile long trim trail and some seventeen miles of paths, and a Visitor's Centre.

Eastwood Lock.

Shipley Lock.

THE NUTBROOK CANAL
- 9 MILES

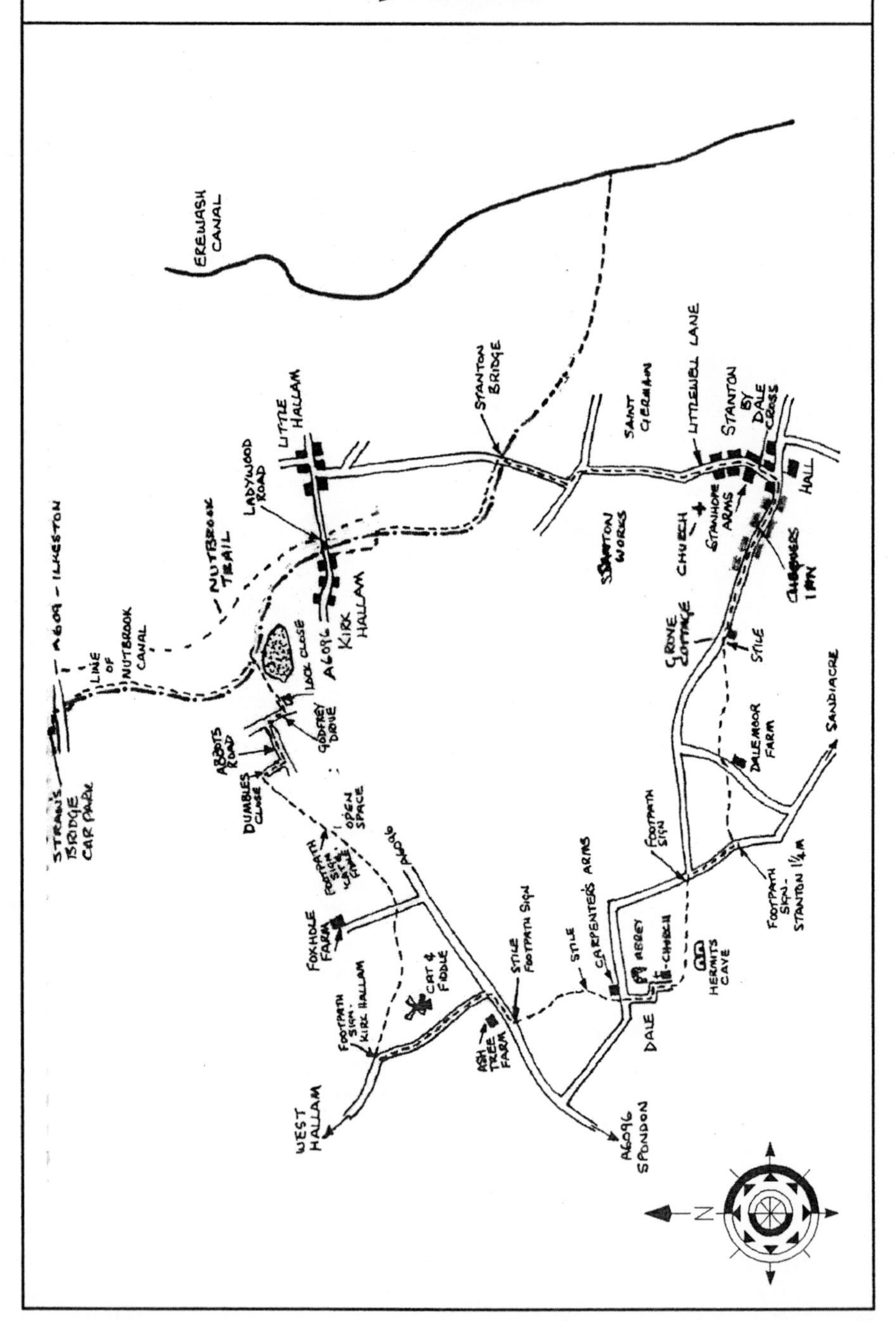

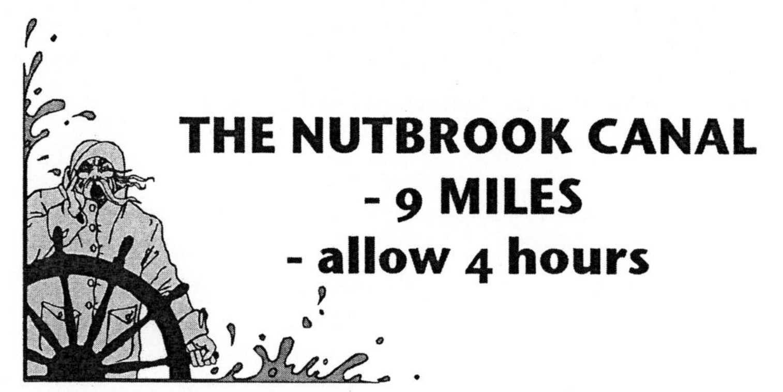

THE NUTBROOK CANAL
- 9 MILES
- allow 4 hours

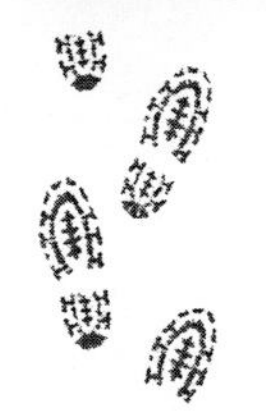

***Basic Route** - Straw's Bridge Car Park - Line of Nutbrook Canal - Kirk Hallam - Ladywood Lodge Farm - Cat & Fiddle Farm - Cat & Fiddle Windmill - Ashtree Farm - Dale - Hermit's cave - Dalemoor Farm - Dale Road - Stanton by Dale - Stanton Works - Stanton Bridge - Nutbrook Canal - A6069 - Nutbrook Trail - Straw's Bridge Car Park.*

***Map** - O.S. 1:25,000 Explorer Series No. 260 - Nottingham.*

***Car Park and start** - Straw's Bridge. Just west of Ilkeston beside the A609 at G.R.453413.*

***Inns** - Carpenter Arms, Dale. Chequer's Inn and Stanhope Arms in Stanton by Dale.*

***Teas** - Dale Abbey Tea-room, Dale.*

ABOUT THE WALK - The route follows the only water filled section left of the Nutbrook Canal, which is a popular fishing section of Stanton Works Fishing Club. First you follow the line of the canal to another lake before walking through the northern edge of Kirk Hallam to pickup the path to the Cat & Fiddle windmill. From here you cross fields to the historically fascinating village of Dale with its ruined abbey, minute church and hermit's cave. Delightful paths lead you to another fascinating village, Stanton by Dale, which has a market cross, water pump, almshouses and a church. You descend past Stanton Works and gain the water filled section of the canal, which you follow northwards to the A6096 road. Here the remains of the canal cease and you join the Nutbrook Trail close to the canal's line and return to Straw's Bridge car park and lake.

WALKING INSTRUCTIONS - From the car park walk around the righthand side of the lake to the Nutbrook Trail; this is your return path. Don't turn right to the trail, keep ahead and turn right through the railway bridge and follow the path to the A609 road, basically on the line of the Nutbrook canal. Cross the road and continue ahead on the tarmaced drive to the Ilkeston Community Technology College. In 1/4 mile as you near a lake turn right on a tarmaced path to the houses of Kirk Hallam. Walk past them on your right to the main road - Godfrey Drive. Turn right passing the aptly named Lock Close on your right. Just after turn right into Abbot Road. In a few yards turn left into Dumbles Close. At house no. 35, turn right along a tarmaced path between the houses. Follow it left and across two roads to reach a road with an open space and play area to the right. Go straight across, as footpath signed, and keep to the lefthand side of field to reach a stile. Continue ahead to gate gap and then keep the hedge on your right. This soon bears left as you continue close to it, with views unfolding. Reach another stile and keep the hedge on your left. Just after go through the hedge to continue with the hedge on your right. Continue on the well stiled path to Ladywood Lodge Farm. Bear right to walk along the righthand edge of the farm to stiles before reaching the farm drive to Foxhole Farm.

Cross to your right to a path sign and follow a grass track uphill past Christmas Trees on your right. later it becomes a path with a hedge on your left. To your left can be seen the Cat & Fiddle windmill. Further gain a hedged track which you descend gently past a house on your left to a path sign, Turn left to the Cat & Fiddle Lane. Turn left and ascend the lane past the windmill entrance on your left and down to the A6096 road. Turn right for 200 yards and just after Ashtree farm on your right, turn left to two oak trees and descend to a stile and path sign. descend the lefthand side of the field to a track. Cross to your left and walk along the lefthand side of the field to a stile and small footbridge. Bear right along the defined path and gain the car park of the Carpenter's Arms. Continue to the main road in Dale and go straight across and descend The Village road in Dale. Follow the road left to pass the Manor House and remains of the abbey. Continue round to your right to a gate and continue on a bridlepath and pass All Saints church. Continue on the wide path which swings left to a gate. Keep ahead through the lefthand side of Hermit's Wood and soon pass the Hermit's Cave to your right. At the end of the wood at a gate, keep ahead along the righthand side of the field beneath the wooded edge, still on a defined path, to a stile and Dale Road.

Turn right and ascend Woodpecker Hill and after 200 yards near the summit, turn left at a stile and footpath sign. Keep a hedge on your left to a stile before crossing two fields via stiles to gain the lane infront of Dalemoor Farm. Turn left along the road and in 50 yards right at a stile and path sign. Reach another stile almost immediately and go through the metal gate beyond. Aim for the solitary oak tree and stile on its right. Continue ahead to the righthand side of a small plantation - pine and oak - to a stile. Here gain a a wide fenced path and walk beside the plantation on your right to a stile. Continue on the level path around the righthand side of the slope before turning left and descending to a stile. Continue right on the path to a stile before Dale Road, with Grove Cottage on your right and lake beyond. Turn right and follow the road into Stanton by Dale, passing the Chequers Arms on your left. Just after at the road junction, turn left on the Ilkeston Road - Stanhope Street. Pass the cross dated 1632, then Stanhope Arms and the water pump, given by the women of Stanton by Dale in celebration of Queen Victoria on June 22nd. 1897. The road, now Littlewell Lane, follow it downhill past Stanton and Bonna Works and Saint Germain Pipes on the right. At the road junction turn left then right, still on the Ilkeston Road, and in 1/4 mile reach the canal bridge. At the lefthand end, go through the metal bollards and walk along the canal towpath with the canal on your left. Soon pass the remains of a lock on your left. the canal turns right through woodland to a former canal bridge. Continue beside the canal and 1/4 mile later reach a footbridge; basically at the end of the visible canal. Turn left across it and follow the path to a football field. Bear right to a road and houses of Kirk Hallam. In the far righthand corner of the field before the houses, below can be seen a canal bridge.

Gain Valley View road and follow it left to the road, St. Norbert Drive. Turn right to the A6096 with Godfrey Drive ahead. Turn right along the main road for a few yards to the former railway bridge and Nutbrook Trail sign. Turn left and descend steps to the trail and turn left - Straw's Bridge is about 3/4 mile away. The trail along a former railway line keeps close to the line of the canal on your left in the trees. Pass under two bridges before turning left and leaving the trail to regain Straw's Bridge, lake and car park.

Remains of the Nutbrook Canal.

THE NUTBROOK CANAL

Authorised in 1793 and opened in 1795. Built by Benjamin Outram, of the Butterley Company, at a cost of £22,800.

The Canal was 4 1/2 miles long and linked the collieries at Shipley (Edward Miller Mundy) and West Hallam (Sir Henry Hunloke's) with the Erewash Canal at Stanton, via Kirk Hallam. There were three reservoirs at Shipley to feed the canal, two - Shipley and Mapperley - of which remain today. Along its length were thirteen locks. mining subsidence involved expensive repairs to the canal leading to its abandonment and by 1890 it was little used. In 1948 the Stanton and Staveley works acquired it and their former factory straddles the site of the canal. The Erewash connection is filled in but on the Erewash Canal the Junction lock remains. A small section towards Kirk Hallam is water filled, with remains of locks and bridges. Beyond Kirk Hallam little remains. Like the Erewash Canal, the Nutbrook Canal had tramway links to collieries.

CAT & FIDDLE WINDMILL - Post mill dating from at least 1788. The stone round house was added in 1844.

DALE - The Abbey was completed in the late 13th. Century and was dissolved in 1539. Little remains today, apart from some of the masonry in the Manor House. Behind is a solitary window arch - 40 feet high by 16 ft wide. The stained glass windows were removed and are now in the north aisle of Morley church four miles away, and are particularly fine. The wooden pews are now in Radbourne church, near Derby.

The church is unique sharing the same roof as the farmhouse. It dates from 1480 and measures 26 feet by 25 feet. The 15th. century Dale Abbey font is inside. The church once married runaway couples in the 18th century. The adjoining farmhouse was for a time an inn.

The Hermit's Cave which has a doorway and two windows, was carved by a hermit between 1130 - 1140 A.D.

STANTON BY DALE - The cross dates from 1632. The church dedicated to St. Michael and All Angels, dates from Norman times, although much of the present building is from the 14th. century onwards. The Norman tympanum is unusual with a circle and cross carved upon it.

THE NUTBROOK TRAIL - 10 MILES - NORTHERN HALF

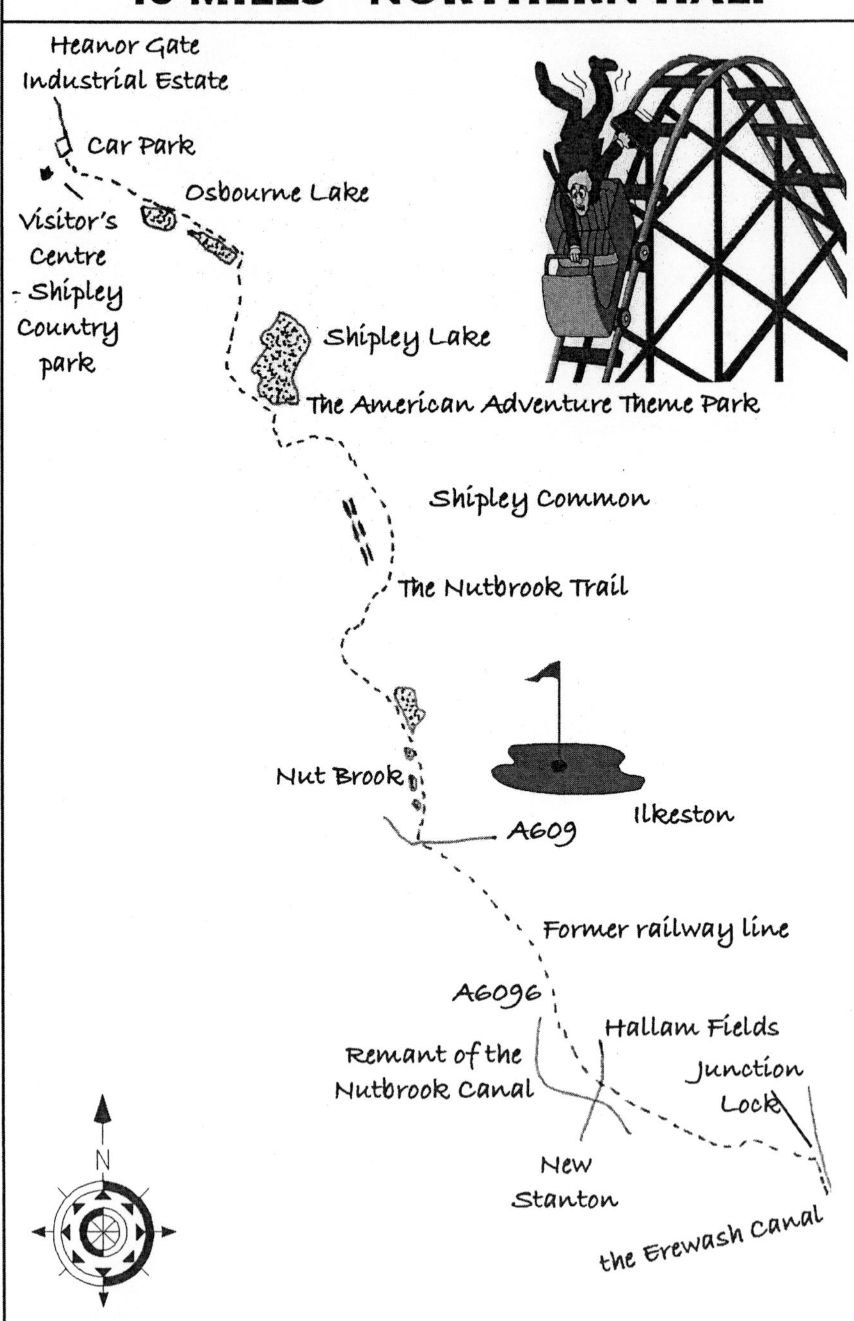

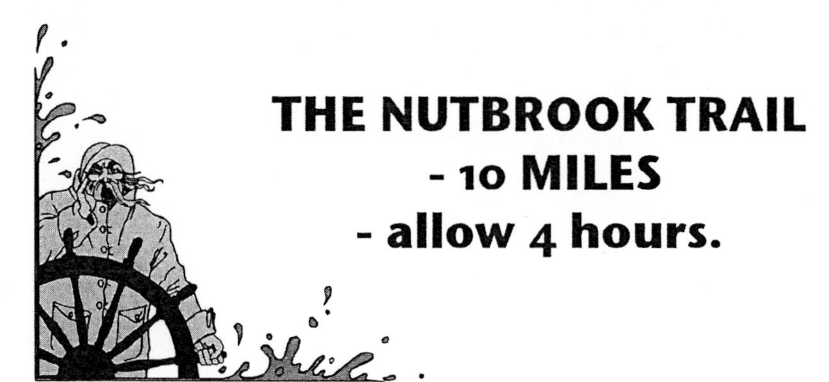

THE NUTBROOK TRAIL - 10 MILES - allow 4 hours.

***Basic Route** - Shipley Country Park - American Adventure Theme park - Former Railway Line, Stanton Branch Line - Nutbrook Canal - Junction Lock - Erewash Canal - Sandiacre - Long Eaton Town Hall.*

***Map** - 1:25,000 Explorer Series No. 260 - Nottingham.*

***Car park and start** - Shipley Country Park, near the Visitor's Centre near Heanor. Grid Ref. 432454. The park is well signed in Heanor.*

***Inns** - just off the route in Sandiacre - the Red Lion Inn and White Lion Inn. Harrington Arms near the end in Long Eaton.*

ABOUT THE WALK - The trail, which is part of a cycle network, follows a former railway line - the Stanton branch line - close to the disused Nutbrook Canal, to Junction Lock and the Erewash Canal. The trail follows the Erewash Canal towpath for more than four miles to Long Eaton. There is no end to end bus service and to get back requires three buses and a journey time of some two hours! The alternative is to leave one car at Long Eaton and the other at Shipley Park. Alternatively, you can like me, walk it both ways making a very pleasant level walk of twenty miles!

WALKING INSTRUCTIONS - From the car park at Shipley park, near the Visitor's centre, starting from the Information Board, follow the path over the brow of the field and down towards the tree lined edge.

Keep left to the trees and bridlepath. Turn right and follow the path soon passing Osborne's Pond on your right. Just after gain a tarmaced surface and cycle path No. 67 - your marker number for the whole trail to Long Eaton. Follow the tarmaced surface for a 1/4 mile to your first Nutbrook Trail sign. Turn right and pass the lakeside Business Centre on your right. Follow the trail down and bearing left up the "hill", passing the first of three metal sculptures of wild weeds - Campion - on your right. At the top descend with the American Adventure Centre and Shipley lake on your left. Guided by the signs bear right past Paul's Arm, still on a tarmaced cycleway, and later left around woodland to a Nutbrook Trail Board. Continue ahead with the houses of Shipley Common on your left and to your right several elongated ponds. In 1/2 mile the trail turns right then left and reached the former Stanton branch line. Continue along this, heading southwards. Pass a lake on your left and then three smaller ones on your right, with a golf course on your left. Gain the A609, and continue along the former railway line through a cutting and under two bridges. Follow the trail past Kirk Hallam on your right and to your right can be seen remnants of the Nutbrook Canal. Nearly six miles from Shipley Country Park (2 hours), reach the road at Saint Galsans Pipelines. Cross as signed and pass an industrial complex and the next wild weeds sculpture - Vetch. On your left is the Erewash canal. Descend to the bridge across it with Junction Lock on your left.

Turn right and follow the towpath beside the canal, on your right, for the next four miles. In 1/2 mile pass pasture Lock and 3/4 mile later pass Springfield's Mill on your left as you reach Padmore Moorings and Sandiacre, with the Red and White Lion Inns to your right. Continue beside the canal past Sandiacre Lock, which is the junction of the Derby Canal - Derby 9 miles. Contniue to the next lock, Dockholme and just after leave the canal side to follow the embankment parallel to it on your left. Follow this towards Long Eaton and the third wild weeds sculpture - Birch. Continue into Long Eaton, past Asda on your left to the Town Hall on your right.

THE NUTBROOK TRAIL - 10 MILES - SOUTHERN HALF

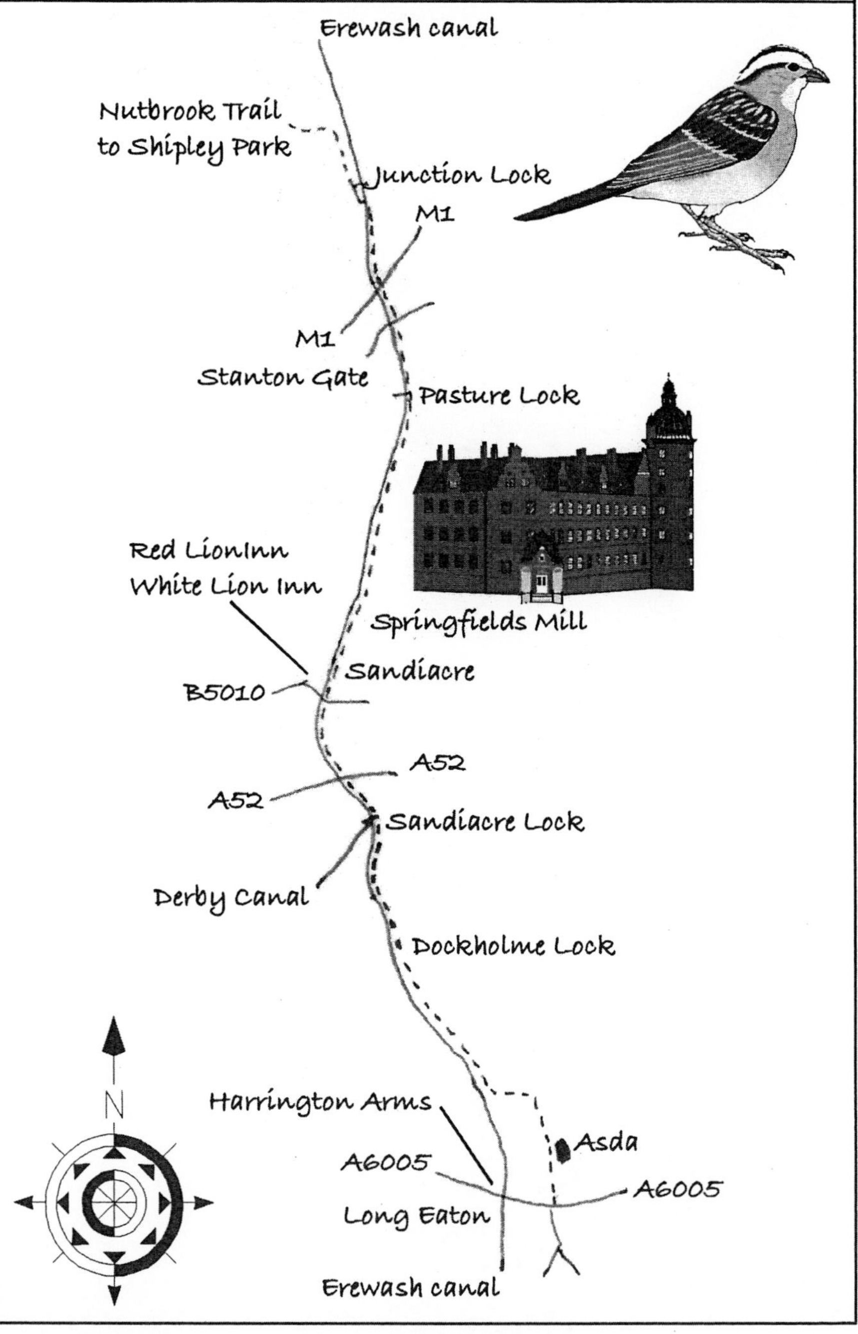

SANDIACRE - EREWASH CANAL - 3 AND 4 MILES

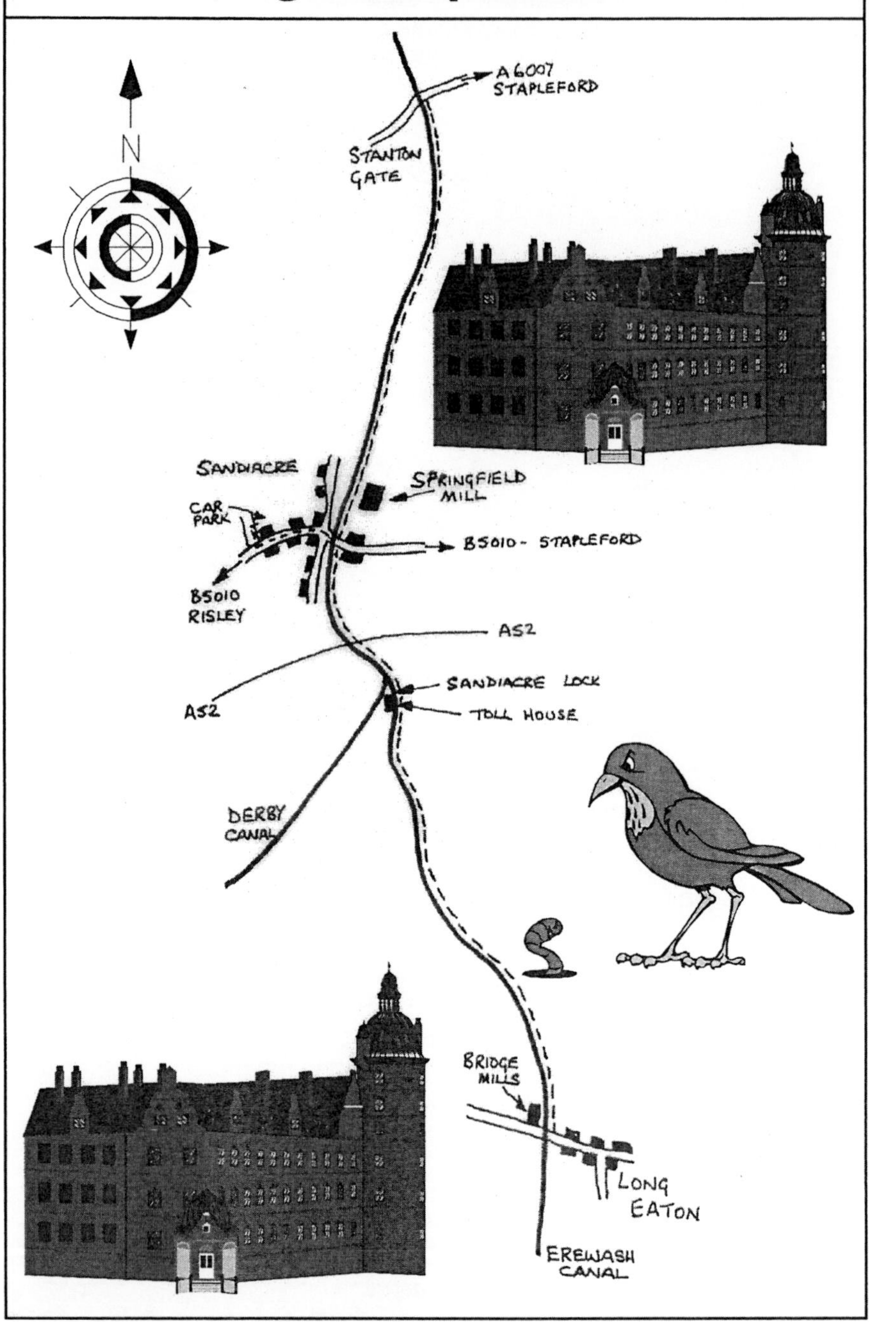

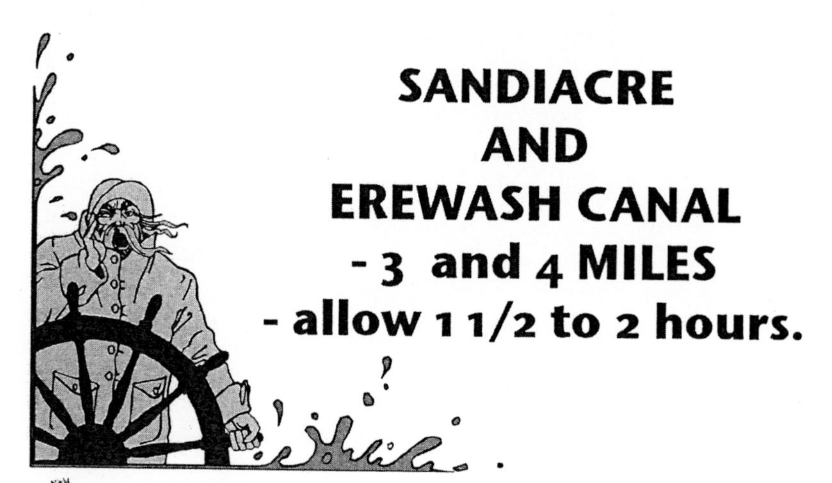

SANDIACRE AND EREWASH CANAL - 3 and 4 MILES - allow 1 1/2 to 2 hours.

Basic Route* - *Sandiacre* - *Erewash Canal* - *Sandiacre.

Map* - *O.S. 1:25,000 Explorer Series No. 260* - *Nottingham.

Car Park and start*- *Road side parking in Sandiacre* - *Derby Road (B5010).

Inns* - *White Lion, Red Lion, Sandiacre. Harrington Arms, Long Eaton.

ABOUT THE WALKS - Sandiacre is ideally situated with some of the most attractive canal walking to the south and north of the town. Despite the housing and surrounding industry, the canal forms a delightful unspoilt and quiet haven through this landscape. To the north is Springfield Mill and the Nutbrook Canal junction and southwards is the junction of the Derby and Erewash Canals, close to the only toll house on the Erewash Canal. Because of the built up area either side of the canal, both these short walk return the same way. The northern route follows part of the Nutbrook Trail and the southern route can be added onto the Long Eaton & River Trent walk, making a 9 mile route or a 7 mile walk to Trent Lock and back.

WALKING INSTRUCTIONS -

North to Stanton Gate - 3 or 4 miles - with the option of continuing a further 1/2 mile (1 mile return) to junction Lock and the start of the Nutbrook Trail. Walk along Derby Road (B5010), eastwards to the canal. Cross the canal bridge and turn left along the towpath with the canal on your left. Walk past Springfield Mill on your right and continue beside the canal, passing Pasture Lock, in a delightful rural setting, after a mile. Continue to the road at Stanton Gate; here you can either turn round and retrace your steps or continue a little further passing under the M1 and onto Junction Lock, 1/2 mile ahead. Return the same way back to Sandiacre.

South to Long Eaton - 4 or 8 miles - Walk along Derby Road (B5010), eastwards to the canal bridge. Cross and turn right onto the towpath, keeping the canal on your right. Pass Padmore Moorings. Pass under the A52 road and reach the junction of the Derby Canal, to your right, beside Sandiacre Lock. The lock cottage dates from 1779. The canal sign sates - Derby 9 miles; Langley Mill 8 miles and Trent Lock 4 miles. Continue beside the canal and in 1/2 mile pass Dockholme Lock and more than a mile later the A6005 road bridge at Long Eaton, near Bridge Mill. Here retrace your steps back to Sandiacre. Alternatively, you can continue beside the canal to Trent Lock, where there are two inns and a tea-room, before returning.

Long Eaton Lock.

The Erewash Canal - view back to Springfield Mill.

The junction of the Erewash and Derby Canals.

LONG EATON, EREWASH CANAL AND THE RIVER TRENT - 6 MILES

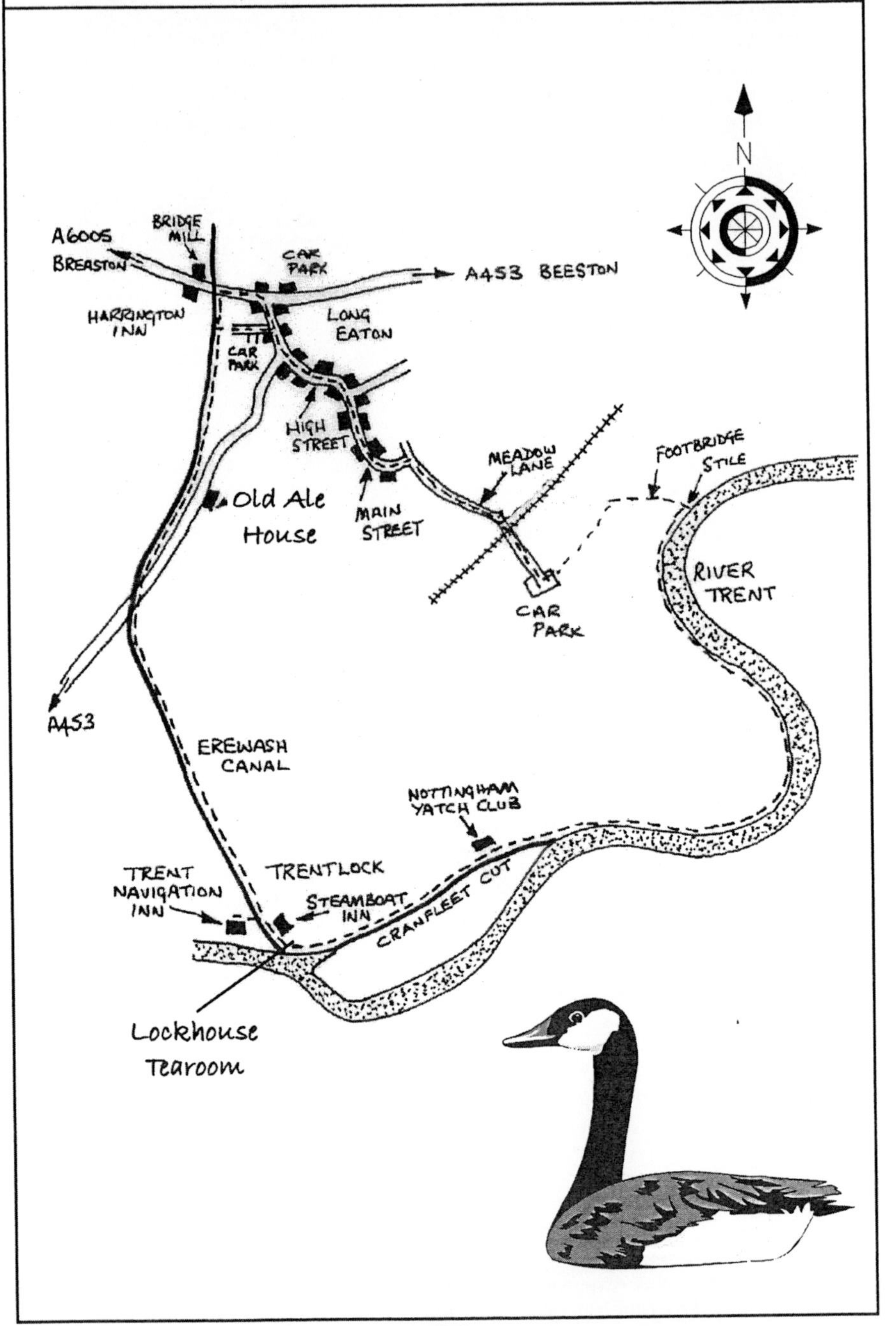

LONG EATON, EREWASH CANAL AND THE RIVER TRENT - 6 MILES - allow 3 hours.

***Basic Route** - Trent Meadows Car Park - Long Eaton - Erewash Canal - Trentlock - River Trent - Trent Meadows Car park.*

***Map** - O.S. 1:25,000 Explorer Series No. 260 - Nottingham.*

***Car Park and start** - Trent Meadows Car park, 1 1/4 south-east of central Long Eaton off Pasture Lane. Grid Ref. 504328. Several car parks - pay and display; 3 hours maximum - in central Long Eaton and close to the Town Hall. You can also start and park from Trentlock, Grid Ref. 491312.*

***Inns** - Numerous in central Long Eaton. Old Ale House beside the Erewash Canal in Long Eaton. Steamboat Inn and Trent Navigation Inn, Trentlock.*

***Teas** - Numerous in Long Eaton. Lock House Tea-room, Trentlock.*

ABOUT THE WALK - The walk can either be started from Trentlock or Long Eaton. I prefer the former as the road section through Long Eaton, linking the River Trent and Erewash canal, is done at the halfway point; leaving a splendid walk along the canal to the River Trent and Steamboat

Inn and Lock House Tea-room. The main thrust of the walk is along the final section of the Erewash Canal to where it joins the River Trent. From here you walk along the Cranfleet Cut, which bypasses the unnavigable river at this point. Following the river for a further mile and you leave it to regain the Trent Meadows Car Park. After walking the canal and its narrow confines it is a contrast to see the wide river and a narrow boat almost lost in an "ocean" of water.

WALKING INSTRUCTIONS - Starting from Trent meadows Car Park, walk back up Pastures Lane, towards central Long Eaton, and under the railway bridge and ahead along Meadows Road. Bear left over another railway line and in Main Street. Follow the road right past Tappers Harker Inn and on past Victoria Inn and into High Street, Keep left, still on the High Street, through the main shopping area of Long Eaton, passing the Blue Bell Inn and the Corner Pin. Reaching the Market Place keep right and pass St. Laurence church on your right, to reach the A6005 road, with the Town Hall and another car park opposite. Turn left and where the road crosses the canal with the Harrington Arms ahead, turn left and descend to the Erewash Canal. Follow the towpath with the canal on your right for the next two miles to Trentlock. Pass the Old Ale House on your left; this was formerly known as the Barge Inn. As you near Trentlock pass house boats on your right. At Trentlock pass the Steamboat Inn and Lockhouse Tea-room on your left and across the bridge to the right is the Trent Navigation Inn. Pass Trent Lock and continue on the lefthand side of the canal and follow the path left away from the river, and continue along the Cranfleet Cut. Pass on the right the Trent Valley Sailing Club. Follow the cut with a magnificent canal bridge near the midway point.

Continue to near its its end and Cranfleet Lock by the club house of the Nottingham Yacht Club. Continue ahead now along the banks of the navigable River Trent for 1 1/2 hours (30 mins), as it loops left. The path is well defined and stiled. After more than a mile begin passing a large lake on your left and soon you can see ahead a semicircular metal footbridge. When almost level with it at a stile, leave the river and cross the footbridge. Continue ahead a short distance before turning left on the second path over the high ground which provides a good vantage point over the area. Follow the path round to your right back to Trent Meadows Car park.

TRENT NAVIGATION COMPANY - Formed in 1783 the company was responsible for maintaining and improving the river between Shardlow and Gainsborough. Proved to be a major waterway route despite competition from the railways. Since 1963 it has been under the control of the British Waterways Board. Today the river is popular with boats, canoeists, anglers, and walkers.

Trent Lock.

The Cranfleet Cut.

DERBY CANAL, TRENT & MERSEY CANAL AND EREWASH CANAL
(THE DERBY CANAL RING WALK - 25 MILES)

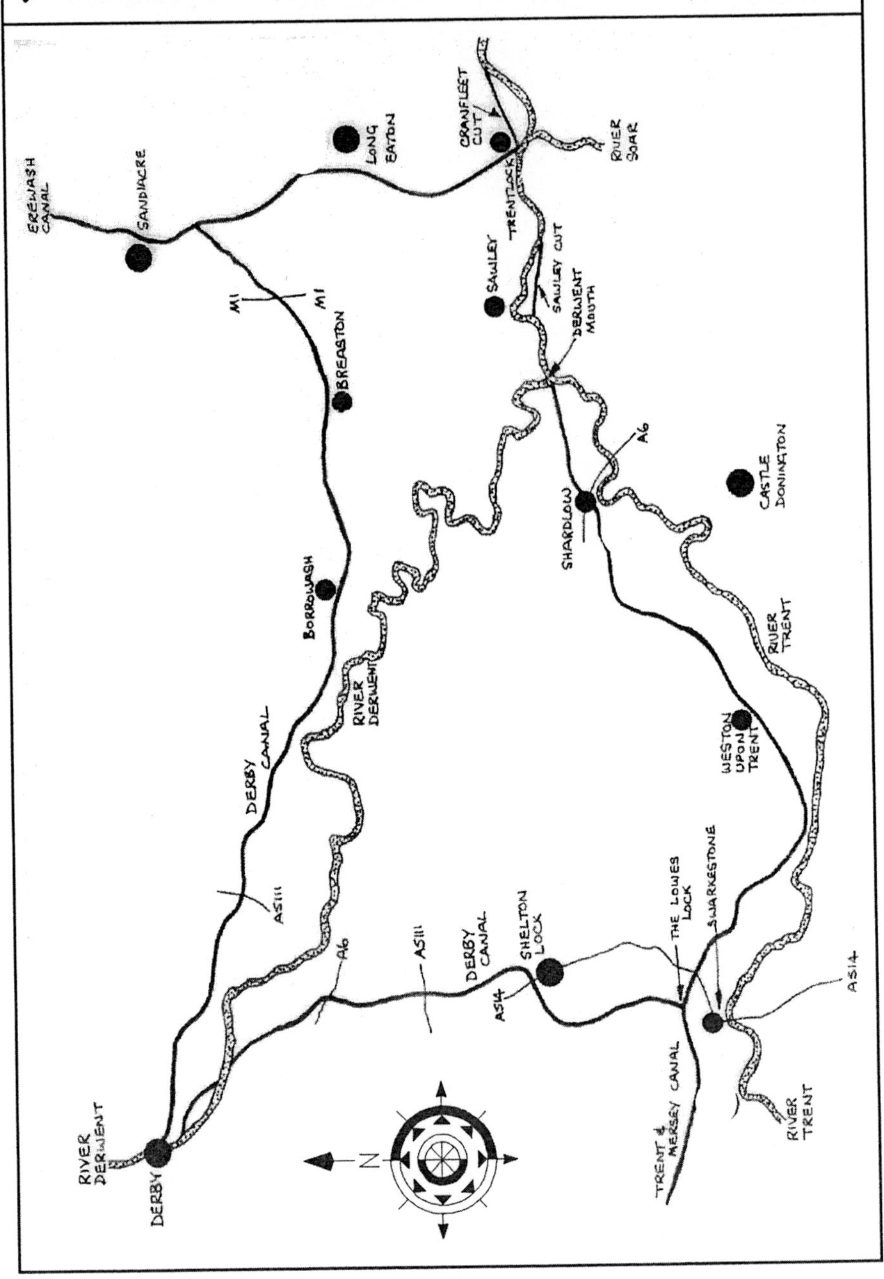

DERBY CANAL
- some brief history notes

Authorised on May 7th 1793 and engineered by Benjamin Outram. It was opened in 1796 and had cost £100,000.

The canal was 14 1/2 miles long from the Erewash canal, south of sandiacre to the Trent and Mersey Canal at Swarkestone. En route passing through Breaston, Borrowash, Spondon, Derby and Chellaston. There were nine locks and in Derby crossed the River Derwent above a 300 foot weir. The towpath was a wooden footbridge known as Long Horse-Bridge, and was demolished in 1959. There were three branches; one via White Bear Lock in Derby, rose through Phoenix Lock to the River Derwent, which was navigable for 11/2 miles to Darley Mills. Another went to Little Eaton, where the 'gang road', a tramroad, led to Denby collieries.

Derby was a major inland port with four large basins. Here the canal was carried across Mill Fleam in the first metal trough (aqueduct) in the country, It was made at Butterley Ironworks in 1795, in five sections - 6 foot deep, 8 foot long at the top, and 9 foot long at the bottom and overall 2 inches thick. The five sections were bolted together.

The Derby Canal Company was privately owned and was never a hugely successful canal because of its high construction costs. It was never nationalised and in 1954 was abandoned. Much of it has been filled in and almost lost, but most sections can still be traced. At the beginning of this century it was little used and after 1935 hardly at all. In its heyday it was popular, and goods arriving at Liverpool started their canal journey at Runcorn Gap and reached Derby six days later. Today, restoration of the canal is in progress.

On the Market day a market boat left Swarkestone for Derby, carrying passengers -

> *".... a market boat, decked over, with seats, and a fireplace, for the accommodation of passengers, starts from Swarkestone every Friday morning, to carry market people to Derby, at 6d each; which again leaves Derby at 4 o'clock for Swarkestone".*

EREWASH AND DERBY CANALS - 9 MILES

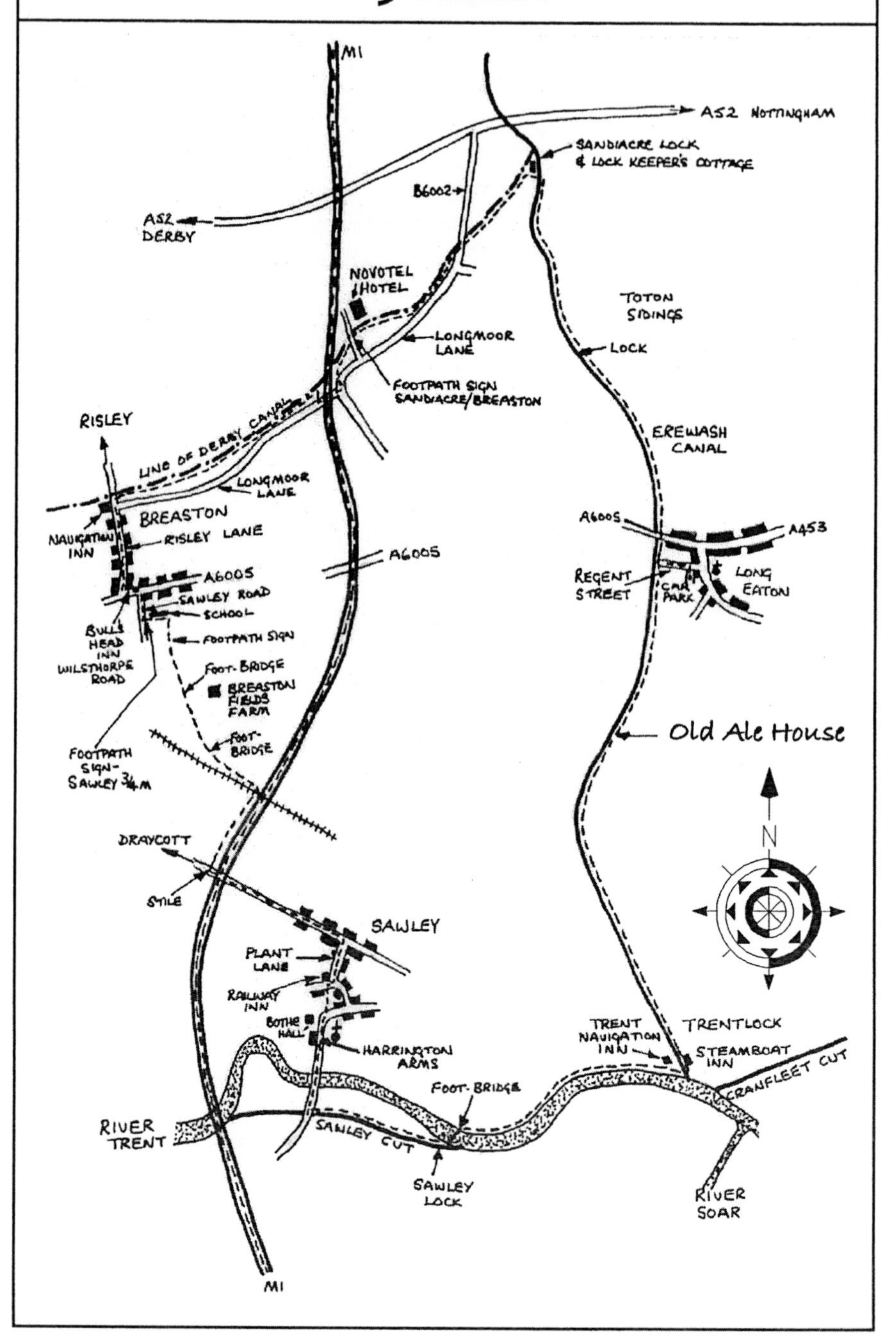

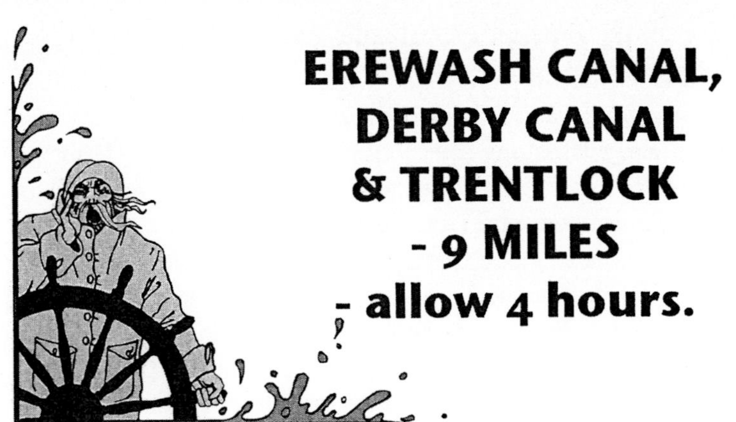

EREWASH CANAL, DERBY CANAL & TRENTLOCK - 9 MILES - allow 4 hours.

Basic route - Long Eaton - Erewash Canal - Sandiacre Lock - Derby Canal - Breaston - Sawley - Sawley Cut - Trentlock - Erewash Canal - Long Eaton.

Map - O.S. 1:25,000 Explorer Series No. 260 - Nottingham.

Car Parks and start - Regent Street, Long Eaton. Alternative at Trentlock.

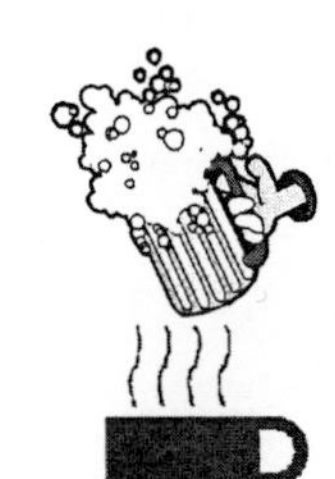

Inns - Numerous in Long Eaton off the route. Navigation Inn, Bull's Head; Breaston. Railway Inn, Harrington Arms and White Lion Inn, Sawley. Trent Navigation and Steamboat Inn, Trentlock. Old Ale House beside the Erewash Canal in Long Eaton.

Teas - The Lock House Tea-room, Trentlock.

ABOUT THE WALK - The walk is a slight misnomer as you will be walking beside three canals. From Long Eaton you follow the Erewash Canal to its junction with the Derby Canal. Then follow nearly three miles along the line of this canal before crossing fields and roads from Breaston to Sawley. Here you walk beside the Sawley Cut on the Trent Navigation and River Trent to Trentlock and the junction with the Erewash Canal. You walk up the canal back to Long Eaton. The walk can be started from the public car park near the Trent Navigation Inn at Trentlock.

WALKING INSTRUCTIONS - From the car park, just off Regent Street, in central Long Eaton, walk back to Regent Street and turn left and follow it to the end, where there is an entrance onto the Erewash Canal. Turn right and walk along the towpath, past the Bridge Mills on your left. Keep on the canal for just over a mile past Dockholme Lock to Sandiacre Lock and prominent pine trees beyond. Turn left over the bridge just infront of the Sandiacre Lock Cottage to the bridge over the Derby Canal. Turn left - footpath signed - Breaston - and follow the distinct path along the line of the Derby canal, past the sites of Sandiacre Top and Bottom Locks. After 1/4 mile pass under the B6002 canal road bridge and bear left along the path, with the road close by on your left. After a further 1/4 mile the path bears right away from the road and continues along to the road close to the M1 ahead. On your right is the Novotel Hotel, Ramada Jarvis Hotel and Brannigan's. Cross the road as bridlepath signposted and continue beneath the M1 bearing left along the edge of the park to the road bridge - Longmoor lane - under the M1 and pass under it. Turn right immediately over the stile by a path sign, and cross the field to the hedge. Turn left and continue straight ahead along the line of the Derby Canal. The next mile (20 mins) is very well stiled and much of the walking is between fences wide apart, illustrating the width of the canal.

Upon reaching the road with the Navigation Inn opposite, turn left along Risley Lane and follow it to its junction with the A6005, 1/4 mile away, beside the Bulls Head Inn. Turn left and 40 yards later right into Sawley Road. 40 yards later pass Firfield Primary School on left and turn left onto fenced path - signposted Sawley 3/4 mile. After 50 yards turn right into a hedged path and follow it to open fields, after crossing a footbridge. Continue ahead across the middle of the field to a stile and across the next to a footbridge. Cross the field strip beyond to the farm road to Breaston Fields Farm, to your left. Cross and continue by the field edge, first keeping it on your immediate right. Cross a footbridge just before the railway and turn left keeping to the field boundary beneath the railway. Just before the end of the field, turn right, through the footpath gate and steps and cross, with care, the railway line. Continue beside the field boundary on your left, with the M1 above. At the end of the field ascend the stile and turn left along Draycott Road and pass under the M1. Follow the road for 1/2 mile to Plant Lane on your right, opposite Sawley Park. Follow this to the road junction beside the Railway Inn. Turn right and left almost immediately, on the right of House No. 54 - Pumpkin Cottage - along the path, to the road - A435 - opposite the Sawley Church, dedicated to All Saints. Turn right beside the road past the Harrington Arms on your right and over Harrington Bridge over the River Trent. Just beyond reach the Sawley Cut and turn left.

Keep the Sawley Marina on your right, across the water, and follow the tarmaced road to Sawley Lock. Just beyond ascend the footbridge over the River Trent and turn right, along the path along the banks of the river. On your left is the Trentlock Golf Centre. A mile later reach Trentlock, with the Trent Navigation Inn on your left, (and public car park) before reaching the Erewash Canal. Cross over the canal and turn left along the towpath past Steamboat Inn and the Lock House Tea-room. Follow the towpath for the next 2 1/2 miles back to Long Eaton. As you near the Bridge Mills, turn right into Regent Street and retrace your steps back to the car park.

Dockholme Lock - Erewash canal.

Derby Canal junction sign with the Erewash Canal.

Sandiacre Lock and Canal Cottage, at the start of the Derby Canal.

The start of the Derby Canal from the Erewash Canal.

The Navigation Inn, beside the line of the Derby Canal at Breaston.

TRENTLOCK AND SAWLEY CUT - 3 MILES

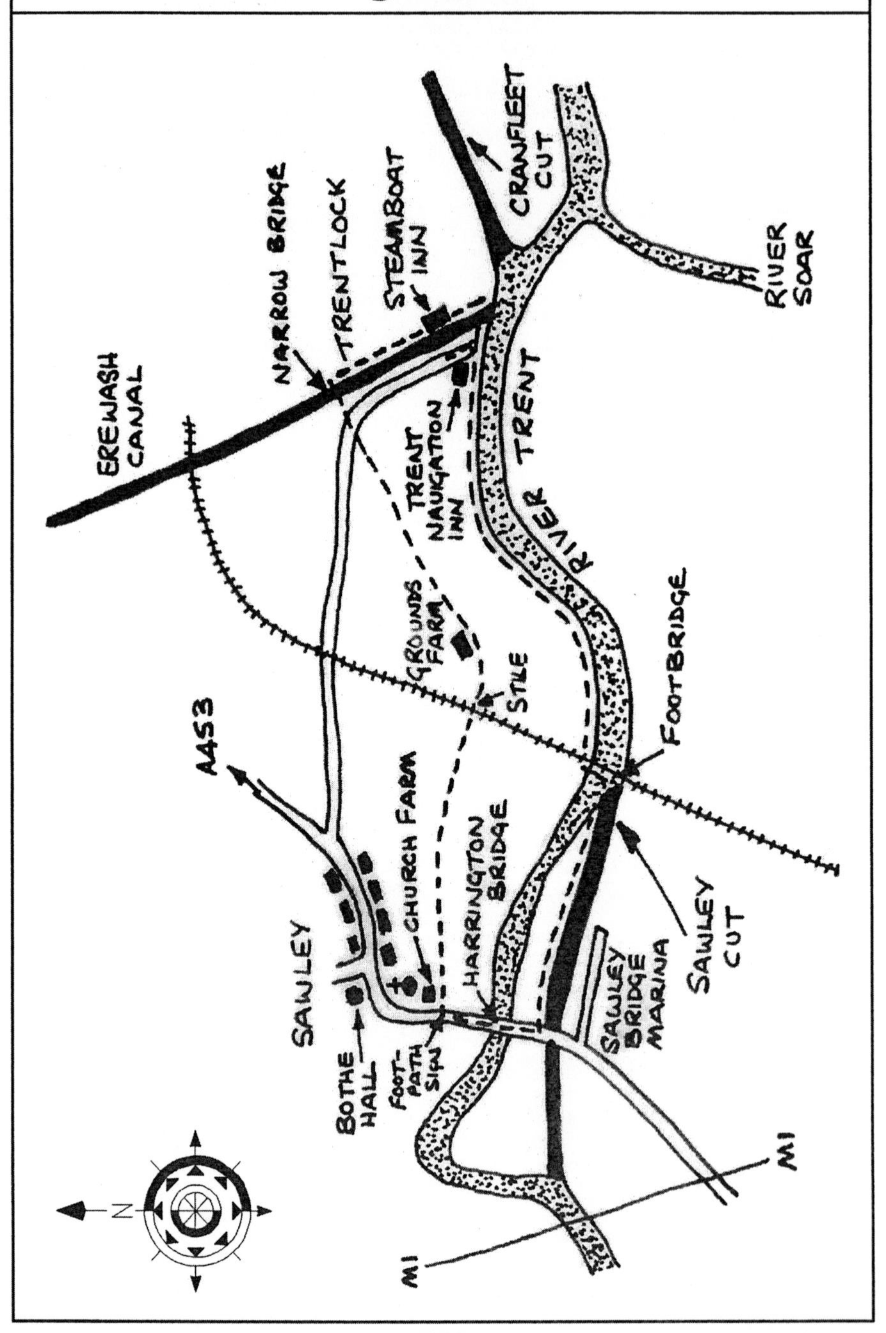

SAWLEY CUT
- 3 MILES
- allow 1 1/2 hours.

Basic route - Trentlock - River Trent - Sawley Cut - Harrington Bridge - Grounds Farm - Trentlock.

Map - O.S. 1:25,000 Explorer Series No. 260 - Nottingham.

Car Park and start - Trentlock. Grid Ref 489314. Reached via Lock Lane off the B6540 road.

Inns - Trent Navigation Inn, Steamboat Inn, Trentlock. Harrington Arms, Sawley.

Teas - Lock House Tea Room, Trentlock.

ABOUT THE WALK - a short walk from the junction of the Erewash Canal with the River Trent along the banks of the river to Sawley Lock and cut. You return over the fields, with an option to explore the village of Sawley, before doing so.

WALKING INSTRUCTIONS - Turn right out of the car park, past the Trent Navigation Inn to the River Trent and turn right. On your left, a short distance away, is Trentlock and Steamboat Inn and Lock House Tea Room. Follow the defined path along the banks of the River Trent for a mile to the railway bridge over the Trent. Pass under the arch before turning left and ascending the footbridge over the river. Turn right at the end past Sawley Lock and along the tarmaced road, past the narrow boats and Sawley Marina on your left. At the road - A453 - turn right and walk over Harrington Bridge, over the River Trent.

Just after and before Church Farm, on your right, is the footpath sign and stile. If you continue ahead you can explore Sawley and see its Church, dedicated to All Saints. Through the stile the path line is along a track beside an earth embankment on your right. The River Trent is far to your right. After 1/2 mile pass under the railway arch and continue ahead along the track to a couple of small ponds on your right. On your right is part of the Trent Lock Golf Centre. On your left is Grounds Farm. Walk past the farm to a stile and continue on a track through the Golf Centre and pass the Club House and car park on your left, to a stile and Lock Lane, 1/2 mile away from farm. Turn left and right to cross over the foot bridge, between Erewash Moorings and Mills Dockyard, over the Erewash Canal. Turn right and walk beside the canal to Trentlock and the Steamboat Inn and Lock House Tea Room. Cross the canal bridge to the Trent Navigation Inn and retrace your steps back to the car park.

SAWLEY - The Church was founded by monks who rowed across the Trent from Repton in 822. Most of the present building is 14th century with some excellent 15th century oak timbers and carvings. There are several monuments to the Bothe family who founded Bothe Hall in the 15th century. Just up the path opposite the church is the house (No 52) where the Rev. John Clifford was born on 16th October 1836. Although only poor he went on to obtain five degrees at London University and became a major Nonconformist.

Sawley Marina.

Sawley Lock and footbridge on left over the River Trent.

CHURCH WILNE & THE DERBY CANAL - 6 MILES

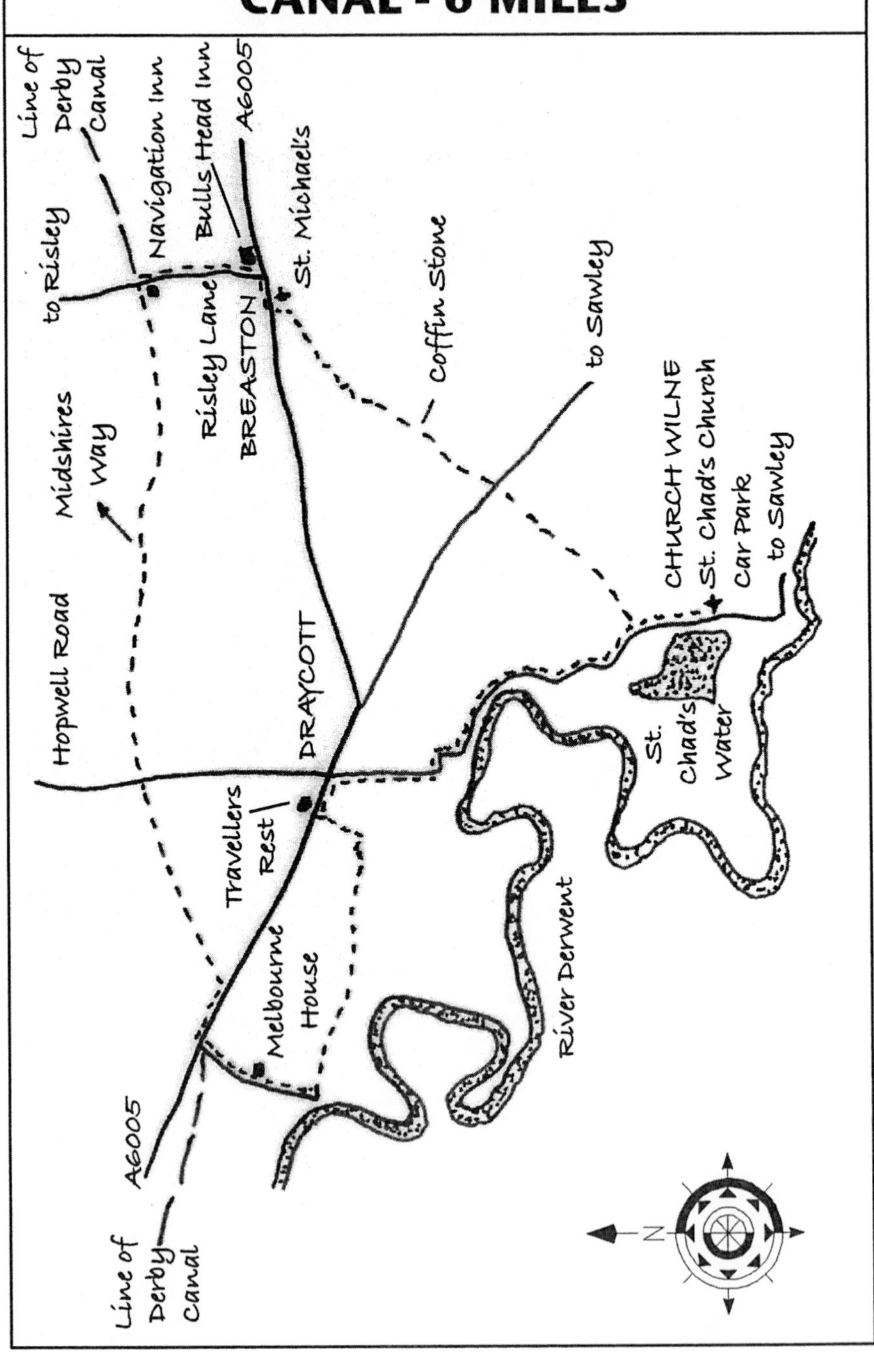

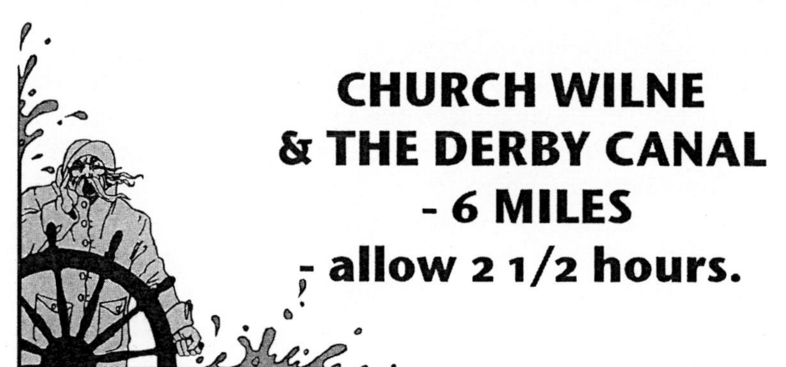

CHURCH WILNE & THE DERBY CANAL - 6 MILES - allow 2 1/2 hours.

Basic Route *- Church Wilne - Coffin Path - St. Michael's church, Breaston - Risley Lane - Navigation Inn - Derby Canal - A6005 - River Derwent - Draycott - Church Wilne.*

Map *- O.S. 1:25,000 Explorer Series No. 260 - Nottingham*

Car Park and start *- Church Wilne, beside St. Chad's Water. Grid Ref. 448317. Alternative opposite the Traveller's Rest Inn in Draycott, off the A6005.*

Inns *- Chequers Inn, Bull's Head, Navigation Inn; Breaston. Traveller's Rest, Rose & Crown; Draycott.*

ABOUT THE WALK - Starting from Church Wilne and its isolated church, the site of a lost village, the route heads northwards along the Coffin path. The two mile section to St. Michael's church, Breaston, follows the route taken by the coffin bearers to Church Wilne before burials took place at Breaston. North of the town at the aptly named Navigation Inn, you join the one of the Derby Canal. You follow the initially restored canal across Draycott Fields to the A6005. Beyond the canal line is only a path and is soon lost as it enters Derby; (there is a magnificent canal bridge near Borrowash.) You head south to the River Derwent before crossing the fields to Draycott and following the single tracked lane back to Church Wilne.

WALKING INSTRUCTIONS - From the car park at Church Wilne beside St. Chad's Water, return to the road and turn left towards Draycott.

In 1/4 mile the road turns left at Derwent Cottage, on the right is the bridlepath to Breaston. Follow the well defined path, keeping straight ahead, and in little over 1/2 mile reach the Draycott-Sawley Road. Go straight across still following the bridlepath and in 1/4 mile reach the Coffin Stone on the right. Here the Coffin carriers rested on their way to Church Wilne. Continue ahead and cross, with care, the railway line. Gaining the end of a lane in Breaston, turn right over a stile and soon left on the well stiled path which brings you to Church View and St. Michael's church. Gaining the A6005 road turn right past the Chequers Inn and left along Risley Road with the Bulls Head on your right. Follow the lane for 1/2 mile to the Navigation Inn on your left. Immediately afterwards turn left onto a tarmaced cycle route No 6 - Derby. This basically runs along the towpath line of the Derby Canal. On the right is the initially excavated canal. Follow the path for 1 1/2 mile to Hopwell Road. Cross over and in 3/4 mile reach the A6005 road. Before gaining the road it is worth keeping on the towpath beneath it to the end of the reclaimed section and see the canal bridge with towpath. Beyond the canal line is just a footpath.

Walk beside the A6005 road a short distance before turning left along Nooning Lane. Pass Melbourne House on your left and continue to the end of the lane with the River Derwent just ahead. Turn left through a stile and keep the hedge on your right to a stile and footbridge. Continue to another stile and onto a footbridge before walking along a hedged path through woodland back to an open field. Keep ahead on the defined path to houses and road - Lime Grove, opposite house No. 43. Turn right along the road. In a short distance at the start of the first road on your left at another house no. 43, reach a path sign and tarmaced path. Follow it to another road in a few yards. Cross over to your right to continue ahead on the path between the houses. At the end turn left on a tarmaced path which curves right to a car park opposite the Traveller's Rest Inn, in Draycott. Gaining the main road - A6005 - turn right past The Green and right along Market Street. Pass The Rose and Crown Inn and continue on this road. After passing the Boathouse on your right it becomes a single track lane beside the River Derwent, at first, and follow it all the way back to Church Wilne almost a mile away.

BREASTON - The church dates from the 14th. century - tower and spire; the rest is 15th. century.

DRAYCOTT - Famous for lace making with the prominent Victoria Mill built in 1907.

CHURCH WILNE - The church dedicated to St. Chad, was once completely destroyed by fire. Inside is an early Norman font, made from a cross. At the time of the Domesday Book this was a thriving community, with a mill, but only the church remains. Evidence of the village can still be seen with considerable ridge and furrow to be seen in the surrounding fields.

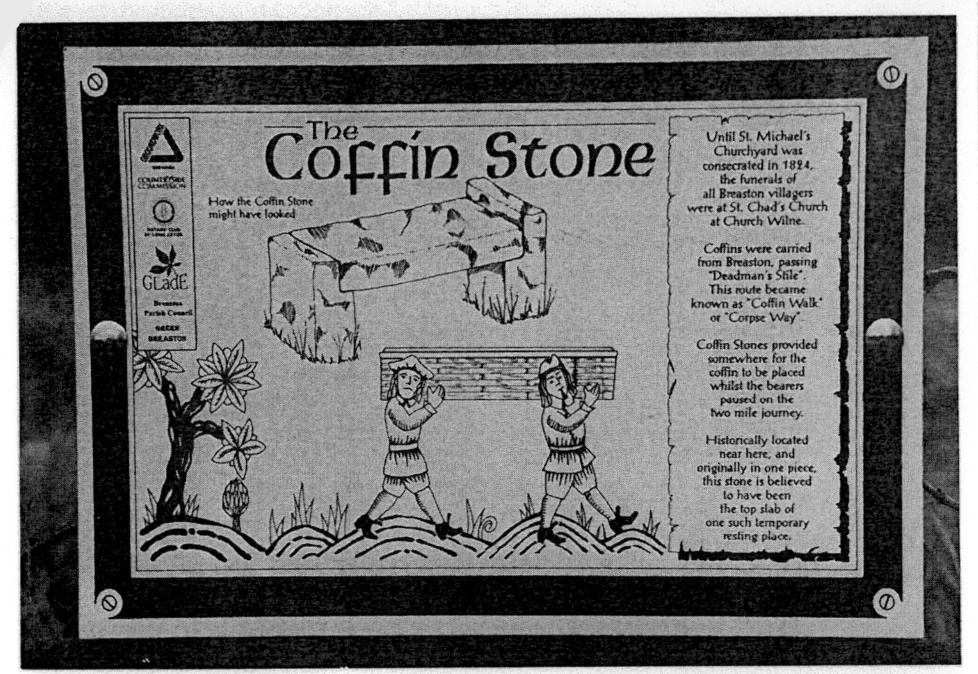

The Coffin Stone.

COFFIN PATH - 2 miles from St. Michael's church, Breaston to St. Chad's church at Church Wilne.

The partially restored Derby canal between the Navigation Inn, Breaston and the A6005.

DERBY & DERBY CANAL, SOUTH
- 3 1/2 MILES - one way.

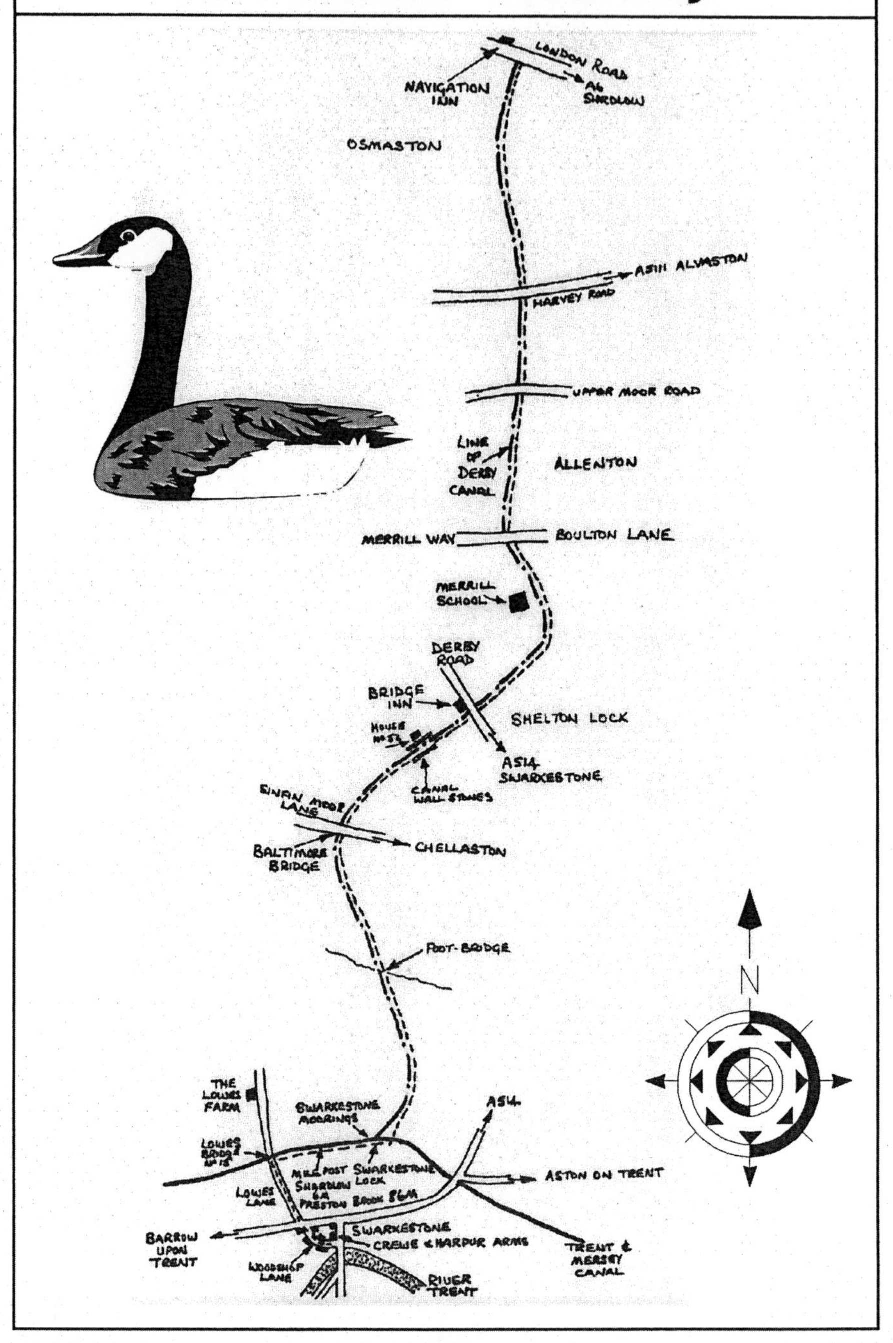

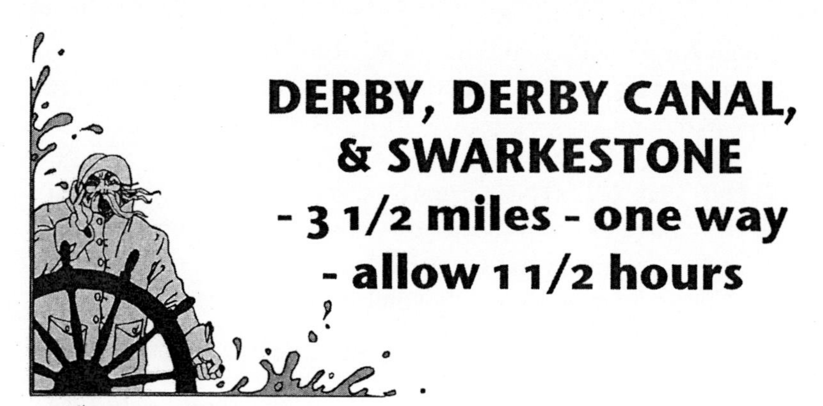

DERBY, DERBY CANAL, & SWARKESTONE - 3 1/2 miles - one way - allow 1 1/2 hours

***Basic Route** - Swarkestone - The Lowes Lock - Derby Canal - Shelton Lock - Allenton - Osmaston - A6, Derby.*

***Maps** - O.S. 1:25,000 Explorer Series Nos -*
- 259 - Derby
- 245 - The National Forest

***Car park and start** - No official one, but space on lanes beside the canal - Lowes Lane and near Swarkestone Lock.*

***Inns** - Navigation Inn, London Road, Wilmorton, Derby. Bridge Inn, Sheldon Lock. Crewe & Harpur Arms, Swarkestone.*

ABOUT THE WALK - From Swarkestone you follow a fragment of the Trent & Mersey Canal to the junction of the now abandoned Derby Canal. Here you follow the line of the canal, at first very discernible to Shelton Lock, before following the basic line of the now filled in canal. Nevertheless an interesting walk into the outskirts of Derby. You can either do it as a one-way walk or return the same way, Swarkestone is worth exploring to see the river Trent and famous Swarkestone Bridge.

You can extend the walk by 2 miles by starting or ending at Derby Railway Station. From here you can walk beside the River Derwent from beneath the Pride Park Bridge and follow the cycle path, for Elvaston castle, for 1 1/2 mile around Pride Park to the railway bridge. The other side turn right and walk through Alvaston Park to London Road and the Navigation Inn. Cross and continue now on the defined line of the canal - see separate map.

WALKING INSTRUCTIONS - From Swarkestone follow Woodshop Lane through the village to the A5132 road. Cross over onto Lowes Lane and follow this over the railway to Lowes Bridge (No 15) over the Trent & Mersey Canal. Turn right at the bridge and descend to the tow path, following for just over 1/4 mile. On the way passing canal milepost - Shardlow 6 miles, Preston Brook 86 miles. A little further on the opposite side of the canal is Swarkestone Moorings. At Swarkestone Lock, turn left over the bridge and follow the track to the bridge over the Derby Canal; turn right just before it and descend to the tow path. The next mile of the canal is attractive walking, being unspoilt and woodland. After 1/2 mile cross a footbridge and 1/2 mile later reach Baltimore Bridge.

From here the canal has been filled in but is well defined and you walk along a good path. After 1/4 mile pass a housing estate on your left and opposite block of houses, incorporating house No. 52, can be seen the exposed tops of the canal. Just beyond pass under the A514 road at Shelton Lock, with the Bridge Inn on your left. The path is now very prominent as you enter more built up area with the Merrill School; no relation to me. named after Merrill Farm that existed here, on your left. Cross the road at Allenton and shortly afterwards keep to your right and follow the canal line over another road before gaining the A5111. Continue ahead for another mile through Osmaston to gain the A6 road - London road. The Navigation Inn is on your left. The canal line can be followed a little bit further but beyond has been demolished by industry. Return the same way back to Swarkestone.

The start of the Derby Canal from the Trent & Mersey Canal.

Merrill School.

View from the Derby Canal Bridge to the Trent & Mersey Canal.

DERBY AND DERBY CANAL - 2 MILES - ONE WAY

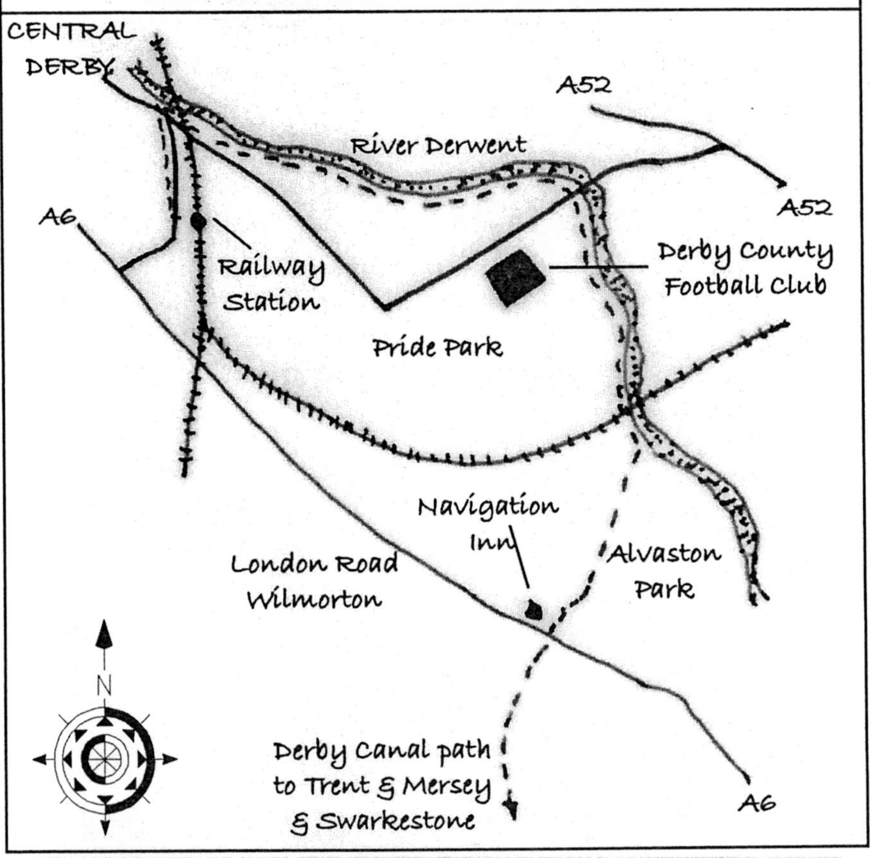

Derby Canal Bridge, near Wilmorton.

Swarkestone Lock, Trent & Mersey Canal, near junction with the Derby Canal.

The solitary Derby Canal bridge near Borrowash.

TRENT & MERSEY CANAL
- some brief history notes

The River Trent had already been navigable to Burton under an Act of 1699. In 1712 4,000 tons of cheese was transported on the river and in 1721 the first boat up the Derwent reached Derby, carrying 'Dale Boards, tobacco, fish and other merchandise'. A canal linking the river Trent to the Mersey was proposed by Erasmus Darwin and Josiah Wedgwood who saw it as a need for the Potteries and Midlands area. James Brindley surveyed the route and it ran from the Derwent Mouth on the Trent to Preston Brook on the Bridgewater Canal near Runcorn - 93 3/8 miles. En route passing through Burton-on-Trent, close to Lichfield, before passing through Rugeley, Stoke and Middlewich to Preston Brook.

The canal - first known as Grand Trunk - was authorised on 14th May 1766 with a capital of £150,000. Work began on the canal immediately but it was not until 1777 that the whole canal was opened, largely due to the problems of the Harecastle tunnel - 2,900 yards long. Many were sceptical that the company would ever pay a dividend but in 1781 5% was paid and in 1825 a £100 share was worth £2,300.

Because of its unique position close to the start of the canal, Shardlow grew into a major inland port. In 1788 the population was 300 and in 1841, 1306. The Trent barges could reach Burton but beyond there the locks were narrow and could only take boats with a seven foot beam. goods going beyond Burton were transferred to narrow boats in Shardlow and vice versa. It is for this reason that there are numerous warehouses and large buildings beside the canal in Shardlow. Associated industries such as boat-building, crane-building, smithying and rope making were all carried on here. The clock warehouse, named because of its central clock, dates from 1780 and now houses a museum. Much of the building has been carefully restored and the basin has been returned to its original state. Shardlow is now, justifiably, a conservation area.

Aston Lock, near Aston on Trent - Trent & Mersey Canal.

SWARKESTONE, DERBY CANAL AND TRENT & MERSEY CANAL - 5 1/2 MILES

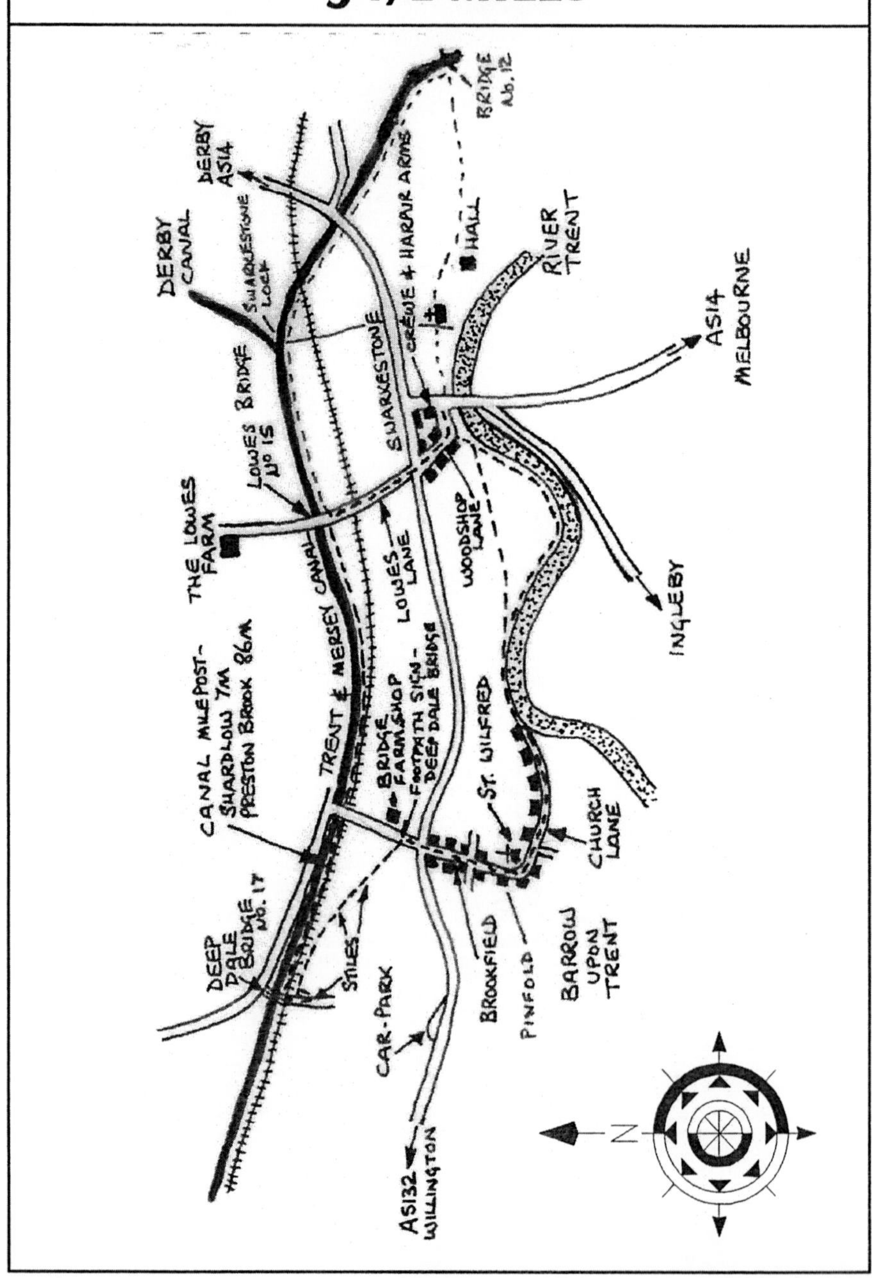

SWARKESTONE, DERBY CANAL AND TRENT & MERSEY CANAL - 5 1/2 MILES - allow 2 1/2 hours.

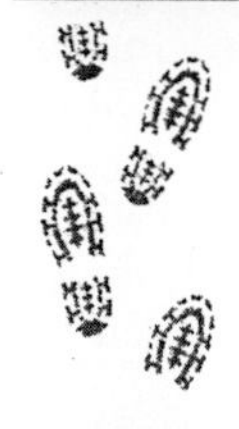

Basic route - Trent & Mersey Canal at Swarkestone Lock - Trent & Mersey Canal - Massey's Bridge No. 12 - Swarkestone Hall - Swarkestone - River Trent - Barrow upon Trent - Deep Dale Bridge No. 17 - Trent & Mersey Canal - Swarkestone Lock.

Map - O.S. 1:25,000 Explorer Series No. 245 - The National Forest - East Sheet.

Car Park and start - Limited roadside parking before Swarkestone Lock, Grid Ref. 373293; reached from A514 road before Swarkestone village. Alternative lane parking close to the canal on Lowes Lane, Grid Ref 368289.

Inns - Crewe & Harpur Arms, Swarkestone. Brookfield's, Barrow upon Trent.

ABOUT THE WALK - A magnificent circuit full of history to places only accessible on foot. You follow more than two miles of the canal, see a remarkable Elizabethan walled enclosure and Swarkestone Bridge, a major river crossing in the Civil War. Later in 1745 it was the most southern point of Bonnie Prince Charlie's abortive attempt to gain the English throne.

WALKING INSTRUCTIONS - Gaining the canal at Swarkestone

Lock turn right along the towpath; to your left is the start of the Derby Canal - 5 miles to Derby. Follow the canal for 3/4 mile to Massey's Bridge No. 12 - just beyond it is the canal milepost - Shardlow 5 miles; Preston Brook 87 miles. Turn right at the bridge and in a few yards right on a defined path. Go through a field gap and onto a bridge. Continue with the hedge on your left to Swarkestone Hall and on the right is the Elizabethan Summer House. Cross the farm/hall drive and pass the Tithe Barn on your left, and cross the field to the righthand side of St. James church, where there is a stile. Gaining the road cross to a path sign and walk past the houses on your left and reach the River Trent, and A514 road, opposite the Crewe and Harpur Arms.

Go straight across and follow the lane - Woodshop Lane - past the inn; on the left in the beer garden can be seen a cairn marking the southern point of Bonnie Prince Charlie's army in 1745. Continue a few yards along the lane to where it turns right with Trent View on the left. Turn left, as footpath signed towards Meadow Farm and left to a stile. Continue along the banks of the River Trent for more than 1/2 mile to a footbridge and along the path to Church Lane in Barrow upon Trent. Pass the Manor House and follow the lane round to your right past St. Wilfred's church and the former Pinfold on your left. Keep straight ahead past Lodge Cottage on your right and on past Brookfield's Inn, in Brookfield's, to the A5132 road. Go straight across into Sinfin Lane and in a few yards on your left is the stile and path - Deepdale Bridge. Cross the field to a stile and onto another. Beyond gain another close to the railway line, and walk close to it to ascend the steps to the railway bridge. Turn right to Deep Dale Bridge No. 17 on the canal, and before it turn right to gain the towpath.

In more than 1/4 mile pass canal milepost - Shardlow 7 miles; Preston Brook - 85 miles. Pass Barrow Bridge No. 16 and soon afterwards the poignant memorial to a boy tragically killed here in 1978, aged sixteen. 1/2 mile later gain Lowes Bridge No. 15. Soon afterwards the next milepost - Shardlow 6 miles; Preston Brook 86 miles. Shortly afterwards is a small canal crane at Swarkestone Stop, for narrow boats. Just after is the junction of the Derby Canal and Swarkestone Lock, where you began.

Derby Canal milepost - 5 miles to Derby - near Swarkestone Lock.

The start of the Derby Canal, near Swarkestone Bridge.

Swarkestone Lock.

SWARKESTONE HALL - Elizabethan Summer House. believed to part of the hall and grounds built by Sir Richard Harpur - one of Queen Elizabeth's judges - and designed by John Smithson who did considerable work on Bolsover Castle. The hall was demolished in the 17th century when the family moved and built Calke Abbey. The family are still remembered in the inn beside the Swarkestone Bridge.

ST. JAMES CHURCH, SWARKESTONE - Contains many monuments to the Harpur family. The tower is 15th. century and inside is a Norman font; in the east aisle wall are fragments of a Norman chancel arch.

SWARKESTONE BRIDGE - The five arched bridge over the River Trent dates from 1796, the remainder almost a mile long dates back to the 14th. century. In 1643 Sir John Gell, the Parliamentary Governor of Derbyshire, routed the Cavaliers here.

BARROW UPON TRENT - The church, dedicated to St. Wilfred, dates back to the 13th. century but much of is 14th. century, including the tower.

Elizabethan Summer House, Swarkestone.

St. James Church, Swarkestone.

LINK PATH - 1 1/2 MILES SWARKESTONE & WESTON ON TRENT WALKS

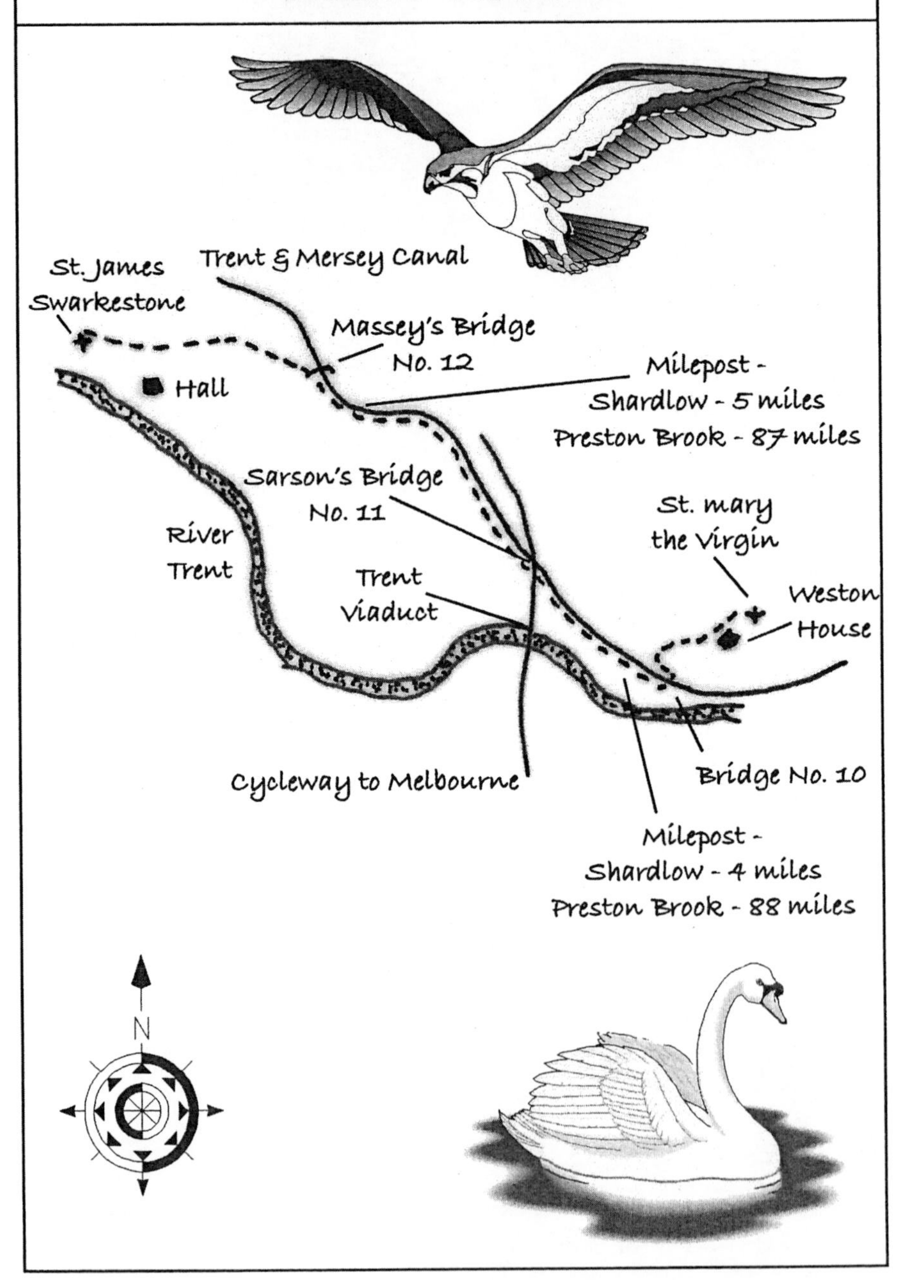

LINK PATH - 1 1/2 MILES (one way) SWARKESTONE & WESTON ON TRENT WALKS

Map - O.S. 1:25,000 Explorer Series No. 245 - The National Forest - East Sheet.

ABOUT THE LINK - Between bridges No. 12 and 10 on the Trent & Mersey Canal, there is no really suitable short circular walk. For those wanting a longer walk of some 12 miles can use this link section to join the Swarkestone and Weston on Trent walks together. Combined they make a wonderful long circular canal walk, full of history, and to some of the unspoilt places of southern Derbyshire.

Using this link all the canal walk from Swarkestone to Shardlow, based on the Trent & Mersey Canal inter link, so you can extend each walk from between six and twenty miles, depending on your plans for the day! ....Happy walking!

WESTON ON TRENT & KING'S MILL - 4 MILES

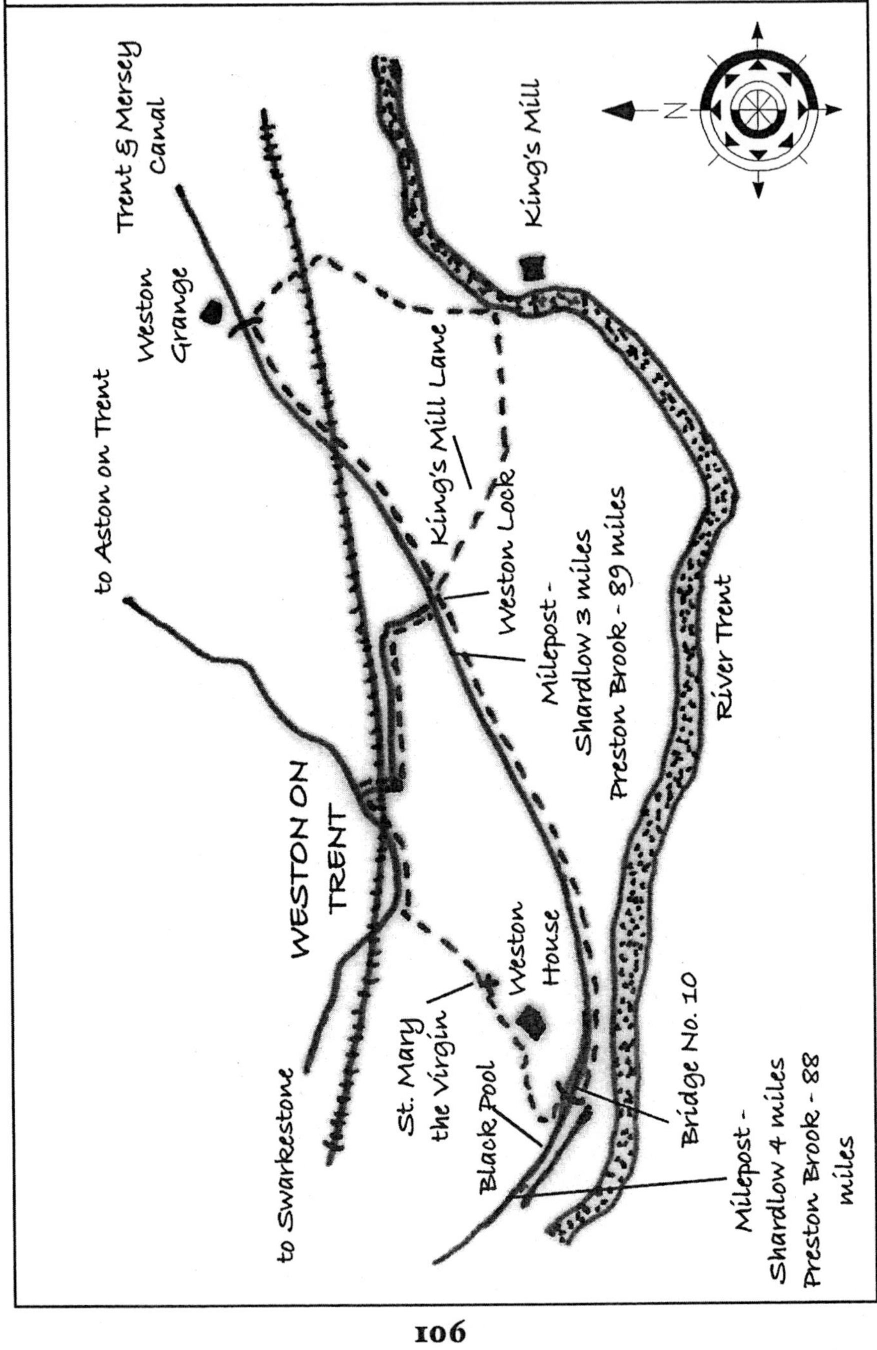

WESTON ON TRENT & KING'S MILL - 4 MILES - allow 2 hours

***Basic Route** - Weston on Trent - King's Mill Lane - Weston Lock - Trent & Mersey Canal - Bridge No. 7 - River Trent and King's Mill - King's Mill Lane - Trent & Mersey Canal - Bridge No. 10 - Weston Church - Weston on Trent.*

***Map** - O.S. 1:25,000 Explorer Series No. 245 - The National Forest - East Sheet.*

***Car park and start** - roadside parking on Main Street, Weston on Trent.*

***Inn** - The Old Plough Inn, Weston on Trent.*

ABOUT THE WALK - A figure of eight walk with Weston Lock at the crossover point. First you walk eastwards along the Trent & Mersey Canal, before crossing the fields to the River Trent, with the King's Mill opposite. You soon rejoin King's Mill Lane back to Weston Lock and follow the canal westwards to footbridge No. 10. A short walk takes you past the impressive Weston Church dedicated to St. Mary the Virgin, before entering Weston on Trent.

WALKING INSTRUCTIONS - Starting from the Main Street in Weston on Trent, opposite the Methodist Chapel, dated 1846, turn left along Trent Lane and cross the railway line before turning left along King's Mill Lane. The lane parallels the railway for 1/4 mile before turning right to the Trent & Mersey Canal at Weston Lock. The lane carries on ahead, which is your return path in another half an hour or so. First, turn left and follow the towpath beside the canal on your left for nearly 3/4 mile to Bridge No. 7, with Weston Grange on the left. Gain the bridge and turn right along a track and just after walking through a railway bridge turn right at a gate, as waymarked - bridlepath. Basically cross the middle of the field aiming for an electric pylon, to locate the next wooden gate. Pass the pylon on the left aiming for a white topped metal post on the banks of the River Trent; opposite is the King's Mill (Hotel) and Leicestershire. At the base of the post is a sign - end of the bridlepath; originally it crossed the river but the bridge has long since gone. Turn half right aiming for the far upper lefthand corner of the field, passing to the left of another electric pylon. Here gain a stile and turn right up King's Mill Lane to Weston Lock.

Turn left and walk beside the canal for a mile, first passing the distinctive Trent & Mersey Canal milepost - Shardlow - 3 miles; Preston Brook - 89 miles. After 1/2 mile pass Scotch Bridge No. 9 and in another 1/2 mile reach a white painted metal footbridge over the canal - Bridge No. 10 - with Weston House and church up on the right. Cross the bridge and follow the path left then right on a tarmaced surface to Weston church. Continue on the lane to Swarkestone Road and turn right, soon crossing the railway line, as you now walk along the Main Road back into Weston on Trent.

Weston Lock.

WESTON ON TRENT - Church dedicated to St. Mary the Virgin. It is somewhat isolated from the village, but originally the village was located here. The impressive church dates from the 13th. century, with the tower and spire 14th. century. The graveyard contains soldiers killed during the Civil War. The Trent Valley saw much activity during the Civil War and Sir John Gell of Hopton Hall, near Wirksworth was the Parliamentary Governor of Derbyshire and took the important and strategic Swarkestone Bridge. Weston House was originally planned as a hall and twice the present size, being started in 1633 by the Roper family. The Civil War put paid to these plans.

The unique Trent & Mersey Canal milepost
- there is one every mile along the canal. This one is near Weston Lock.

The idyllic Trent & Mersey Canal, near Bridge No. 10.

Shardlow Lock.

SHARDLOW, ASTON ON TRENT & TRENT & MERSEY CANAL - 5 MILES

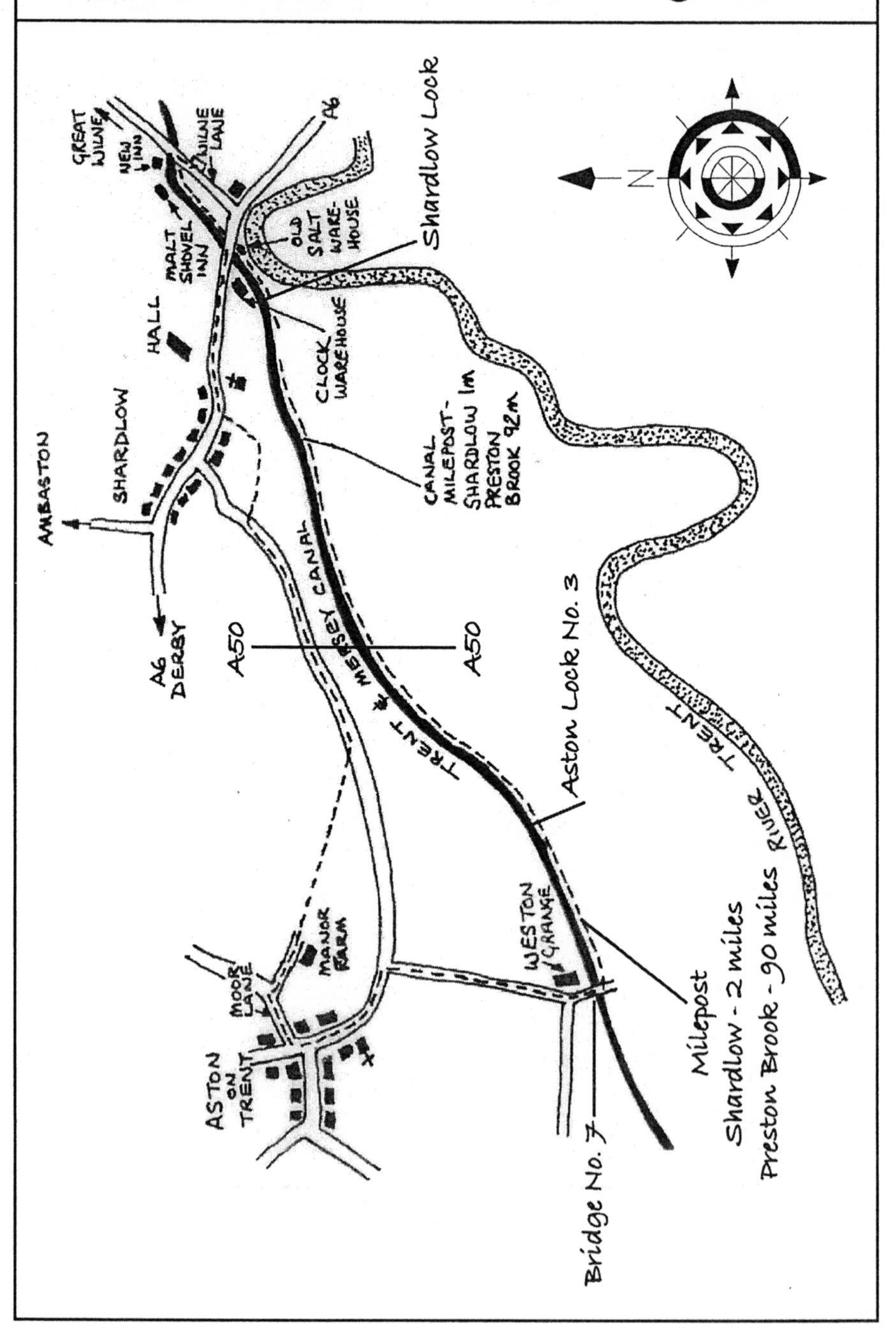

SHARDLOW AND ASTON ON TRENT - 5 MILES - allow 2 1/2 hours.

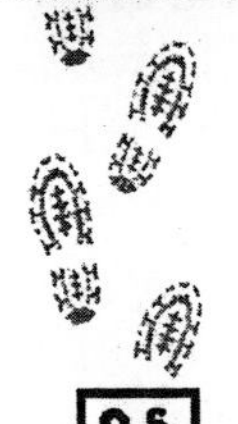

Basic Route* - *Shardlow* - *Trent & Mersey Canal* - *Weston Grange* - *Aston on Trent* - *Shardlow.

***Maps* - *O.S. 1:25,000 Explorer Series Nos* -**
- *260* - *Nottingham*
- *245* - *The National Forest*

Car park and start* - *Shardlow* - *off Wilne Lane* - *Long Stay Car Park.

Inns* - *New Inn, Malt Shovel, Navigation Inn, Shakespeare Inn and Clock Warehouse, Shardlow. The White Hart Inn, Malt Shovel Inn, Aston on Trent.

Teas* - *Canal Bank Tea-room, Shardlow, by Bridge No. 3.

ABOUT THE WALK - First you explore the canal wharfs and warehouses of Shardlow before following the canal to Weston Grange, more than 2 miles away. You can either return the same way or follow the paths and road to Shardlow via Aston on Trent. The latter gives you the option to explore Shardlow further by seeing its Hall,Church and Heritage Centre.

WALKING INSTRUCTIONS - From the car park turn right along

Wilne Lane to the bridge (No 2) over the canal. Just before it turn left to the towpath and keep the canal on your righthand side. After a little over 1/4 mile reach the A6 road bridge. It is worth ascending to the road, crossing it and descending to the canal again. Where you leave the A6 road, on your right, as recorded on the plaque, is 'The Old Salt Warehouse'. On your right is the Clock Warehouse, and Heritage Centre which you explore on your return.

Pass Shardlow Lock, No. 2, and the canal milepost - 'Shardlow 1 mile, Preston Brook 92 miles'. Follow the canal for 2 1/2 miles, passing Aston Lock No. 3, until you reach Bridge No. 7 over it. Ascend to this and cross to your right to Weston Grange. Just past the building turn right and walk up the track to Aston on Trent, 1/2 mile away. At the road turn left to the Church, dedicated to All Saints. Beyond at the cross roads, continue ahead - Derby Road - and pass the White Hart Inn and take the second road on your right -'Moor Lane'. Shortly afterwards turn right - Manor Farm Road - and in a few yards left on a track, a signposted path, across the fields to Shardlow road. Reach a stile and onto a wooden flat bridge. Cross the field to the far upper corner and stile and path sign before Moorside Cottages. Turn left and in a few yards right over a stile. Keep to the righthand side of the field to Shardlow Road. Turn left and follow the road for 3/4 mile, crossing over the A50, to near the boundary sign of Shardlow. Turn right into Aston Lane and immediately left down steps to a stile. Follow the path a short distance to a stile on your right. Over keep the hedge/fence on your left to near a red bricked wall. Well before it turn left over the footbridge and keep to the lefthand side of the field along a path before walking between the houses to central Shardlow and the A6 road. Turn right to pass the Church, dedicated to St. James on your right and Hall on your left. Continue on the A6 past the Shakespeare Inn and back to the canal, with the Clock Warehouse on your right. Retrace your steps along the canal to your left to canal Bridge No. 2 with the Malt Shovel Inn on your left and turn right along Wilne Road back to the car park.

The heavily buttressed tower of All Saints, Aston on Trent.

ASTON ON TRENT - All Saints Church dates from Norman times but is largely 13th and 15th century. The clerestory is 15th century and the font 13th century.

SHARDLOW - was a major inland port, and boats operating in the Derbyshire section of the canal carried up to 40 tons of goods. Until 1785 the boats were hauled by men and from then onwards by horses. There was a stable for 100 horses here and the rope walk still remains. Shardlow Hall was built by Leonard Fosbrooke, a carrier, in 1684.

The Clock Warehouse, Shardlow.

SHARDLOW AND THE TRENT & MERSEY CANAL - 3 MILES

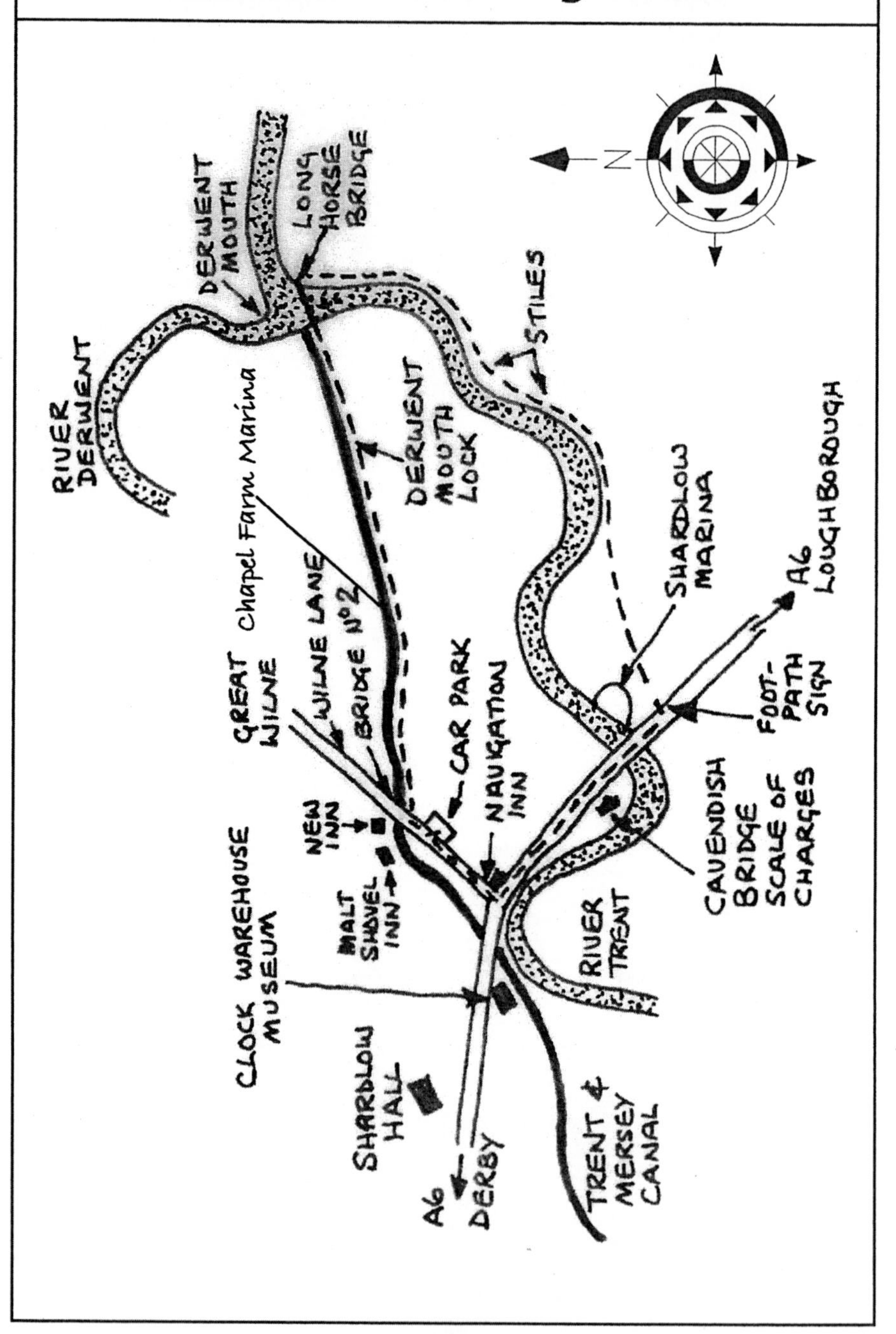

SHARDLOW - 3 MILES - allow 2 hours

***Basic route** - Shardlow - Trent & Mersey Canal - Derwent Mouth - Long Horse Bridge - River Trent - A6 - Cavendish Bridge - Shardlow.*

***Maps** - O.S. 1:25,000 Explorer Series Nos.*
- 260 - Nottingham
- 245 - The National Forest

***Car park and start** - Shardlow, off Wilne Lane - Long Stay car park.*

***Inns** - The Clock Warehouse, Navigation Inn, Malt Shovel Inn and New Inn, Shardlow. Old Crown Inn in Cavendish Bridge, just off the route. The Old Marina, Shardlow Marina, just off the route.*

***Teas** - Near Bridge No. 3 - The Canal bank Tea-room.*

ABOUT THE WALK - Shardlow is one of the finest and best preserved inland ports in England. This short walk follows the Trent & Mersey Canal through Shardlow to the junction of the river Trent and Derwent. You walk beside the Trent back to Shardlow, to allow time to explore fully the port, the Clock Warehouse and Shardlow Heritage Centre.

WALKING INSTRUCTIONS - Turn right out of the car park along Wilne Lane to Bridge No 2 over the canal. Turn left before the bridge and descend to the canal towpath; opposite is the Malt Shovel and New Inn. Turn right and follow the towpath for almost a mile to the rivers Trent and Derwent. Pass Chapel Farm marina on your left and pass under Bridge

No. 1, and after 3/4 mile pass the Derwent Mouth Lock. Cross the footbridge over the river Trent (Long Horse Bridge) and turn right. Walk along the banks of the river Trent for almost 3/4 mile to where the river turns sharp right. Here continue straight ahead across the field to a stile and footpath sign on the immediate left of a large building complex - small Industrial estate - on your right; on your left are lakes.

Over the stile and gain the A6 - London Road - and turn right over the Cavendish Bridge with Shardlow Marina on your right. Continue on into Shardlow and South Derbyshire, passing the plaque on your left of the scale of charges used on the bridge. Pass the entrance to Wilne Lane an the Navigation Inn to reach the canal. The towpath as signed is on your right, but before following it turn left along the lane past the Old Salt Warehouse and onto Shardlow Lock with the Clock Warehouse on your right. Turn right and follow the towpath under Bridge No. 3 and on along it to Bridge No 2 and ascend back to Wilne Lane. Turn right back to the car park.

(2017 Update - New bridge now installed.)

PLEASE NOTE - At the time of writing in April 2004, the Long Horse Bridge is being replaced and is currently closed until November 2004.

The site of Long Horse Bridge.

Malt Shovel Inn, Shardlow.

Derwent Mouth Lock.

Cavendish Bridge Tolls.

Shardlow Marina.

The Navigation Inn, Shardlow.

The New Inn, Shardlow.

WALK RECORD CHART

Date walked -

NOTTINGHAM CANAL -

Nottingham Canal - Brief History Notes ....

Cossall - Nottingham and Erewash Canals - 9 1/2 miles ....

Cossall - Nottingham and Erewash Canals - 3 miles ....

Nottingham Canal, Bramcote and Stapleford Hills - 4 miles ....

Nottingham Canal in Nottingham - 3 miles ....

BEESTON CANAL -

Beeston Canal - brief history notes ....

Attenborough, River Trent & Beeston canal - 4 1/2 miles ....

Beeston canal and Lock - 3 miles ....

Beeston Canal and Nottingham Canal - 4 1/2 miles ....

Beeston Canal, Nottingham Canal and the River Trent - 14 miles ....

EREWASH CANAL -

Erewash Canal - some brief history notes ....

Shipley park, Great Northern Basin and the Erewash Canal - 7 miles ....

The Nutbrook Canal - 9 miles ....

THE JOHN MERRILL CANAL WALK BADGE

Complete six walks in this book and get the above special embroidered badge and special signed certificate. Badges are Blue cloth with lettering and lock embroidered in four colours.

BADGE ORDER FORM

Date walks completed...

NAME ....

ADDRESS ....

....

Price: £6.00 each including postage, packing, VAT and signed completion certificate. Amount enclosed (Payable to The John Merrill Foundation) ..
From: THE JOHN MERRILL FOUNDATION,
32, Holmesdale, Waltham Cross, Hertfordshire EN8 8QY

HAPPY WALKING T SHIRT - white & 4 colours - £10.00

e-mail - marathonhiker@aol.com
www.johnmerrillwalkguides.co.uk

********** *YOU MAY PHOTOCOPY THIS FORM* ***********

CANAL FEATURES TO LOOK FOR -

STOP PLANKS - In various places can be seen vertical grooves in the canal walls - especially near bridges - with handled planks stacked nearby. The planks are slotted into the grooves sealing the canal while repairs or cleaning of a drained section is carried out.

ROPE GROOVES - on the side of the bridges, sometimes with either cast iron or wooden shields, can be seen the grooves cut by the horse tow lines over the decades. A memory of how boats were carried along the canal.

TURNOVER/CROSSOVER BRIDGES - In a few places the towpath switches sides of the canal and a bridge was built to enable the horse to cross over without unhitching the line.

SWING BRIDGES - As the name implies, the bridge could be swung out across the canal or swung to the side to allow boats to pass.

BALANCED BRIDGES - Bridges finely balanced that can be either pushed upwards out of the way or lowered across the canal for people, tractors and cattle to cross.

SKEW BRIDGES - Most canal bridges are built at right angles to the canal. In a few cases to avoid the Z bend in the road, the bridge was built at an angle.

MILEPOSTS - Not every canal has mileposts, but there are path signs giving the mileage. The Trent and Mersey Canal has their own and distinct mileposts, showing the mielage from Shardlow and Preston Brook..

LOCK AND BRIDGE NUMBERS - Not every Canal/Navigation numbers them; many just rely on their name.

POUND - The length of canal between two locks.

WINDING HOLE - A small area/arm of the main canal, usually near a lock, for turning the narrowboat round.

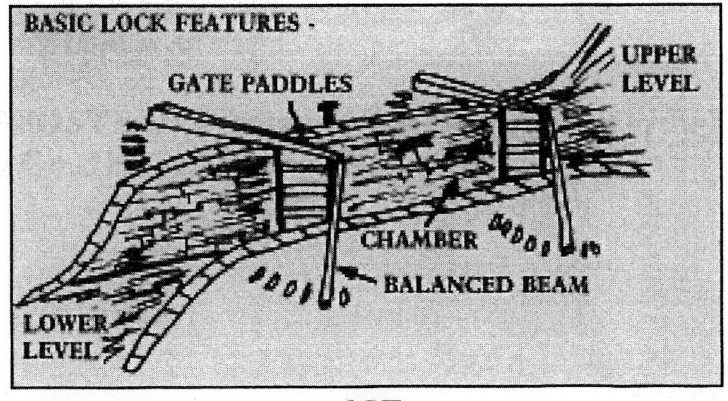

OTHER CANAL WALK GUIDES

by John N. Merrill

VOL ONE - DERBYSHIRE AND NOTTINGHAMSHIRE - More than 30 walks, both short and long, on the Erewash, Derby, Trent & Mersey, Nottingham, Beeston and Nutbrook canals. The guide is not just a walk guide but a historical guide to what can be seen today and a photographic essay to canals in the area. 128 pages 60 photographs 32 maps
ISBN 1-903627-53 -2 £10.95 - wire bound **new enlarged edition**

VOL TWO - CHESHIRE AND STAFFORDSHIRE - Details more than 40 circular walks on the Peak Forest, Macclesfield Caldon and Trent & Mersey canals. Like Vol. 1, a major reference source to canal walking on the western side of the Pennines. All are circular and include both long and short walks with numerous pubs along the way. 88 pages 61 photographs 27 maps ISBN 0 907496 38 5 Wire bound. £8.95

VOL THREE—STAFFORDSHIRE - 36 short circular walks on the Trent & Mersey, Coventry, Staffordshire & Worcestershire Canals within the boundary of Staffordshire, between Stoke on Trent and Burton Upon Trent. This book links together Vol. 1 & 2 of the series. 84 pages 60 photographs 30 maps ISBN 0 907496 62 8 Wire bound £8.95

VOL FOUR—THE CHESHIRE RING - Walk guide with history notes to the 97 mile walk around the ring on the Macclesfield, Peak Forest, Ashton, Rochdale, Bridgewater, and Trent & Mersey Canals. Comprehensive amenities guide to enable you to walk it in stages or as a weeks walk. 80 pages 38 photographs 15 maps ISBN 1-903627-39-7 £8.95 wire bound.
New edition

VOL FIVE—THE GRANTHAM CANAL More than fifteen walks on the Grantham Canal, from the River Trent to Grantham. Unspoilt walking in the Vale of Belvoir. 96 pages 45 photographs 16 maps
ISBN 1-903627-56-7 £9.95 NEW

WALKING THE TRENT & MERSEY CANAL - Walk guide to the whole length of the canal—end-to-end—from Preston Brook to Shardlow and Derwent Mouth. 93 miles of some of the finest canal walking in Britain. Amenities guide and walk described in stages. 64 pages 35 photographs 18 maps ISBN 1 874754 19 5. £6.95

WALKING THE LLANGOLLEN CANAL A complete end to end walk from Nantwich to Llangollen -50 miles, along the canl. The scenery is oustanding and the canal features are unsurpassed. ISBN 1 84173 017 3 56 pages. 25 photographs. 10 maps. £5.95

WALKING THE DERBY CANAL RING - A magnificent 28 mile walk from the centre of Derby, following the line of the Derby Canal to the Trent & Mersey Canal and onto the River Trent and Erewash Canal. You return to Derby along the line of the Sandiacre section of the Derby Canal. ISBN 1874754 28 4. 32 pages. 5 maps. 10 photographs. £4.95

THE SALT & SAILS TRAIL by David Burkhill Howarth. - A magnificent 20 mile walk from Weston Point to Winsford along the Weaver Navigation in Cheshire, with very detailed history notes. ISBN 1 874754 58 6. 44 pages. 7 maps. 10 photographs. £5.95
.

SHORT CIRCULAR WALKS IN THE CHESTERFIELD CANAL More than fifteen walks on the Chesterfield Canall, from Chesterfield via Worksop to the River Trent at West Stockwith. Unspoilt walking Derbyshire & Nottinghamshire. 112 pages 45 photographs 16 maps ISBN 1-903627-56-7 £10.95. Colour edition £14.95. Wire bound.

SHORT CIRCULAR WALKS ON THE CROMFORD CANAL Ten walks on the Cromford Canal, from Cromford to the Great Northern Basin at Langley.. Unspoilt walking, tracing the abandoned canal and Pinxton Arm. 96 pages 45 photographs 16 maps ISBN 1-903627-54-0 £8.95. Colour edition £10.95 Wire bound.

SHORT CIRCULAR WALKS ON THE RIVER LEE NAVIGATION - (London to Hertford) - Northern Volume.
60 pages, 23 photographs, 10 detailed maps and walks - walks between Ponders End Lock and Hertford. History notes. ISBN 1-903627-68-0 £7.95 **NEW**

SHORT CIRCULAR WALKS ON THE RIVER STORT NAVIGATION
Despite only being 13 1/2 miles long from the River Lee Navigation, near Broxbourne to Bishop's Stortford, the navigation is a gem and full of history. Eight circular walks explore its full length and one explores it end to end. The guide is not just a walk one, but a history of the canal and surrounding villages and a photographic essay.
92 pages, 68 colour photographs, 12 maps. Wire bound.
ISBN 1-903627-73-7 £10.95 **NEW**

SHORT CIRCULAR WALKS ON THE RIVER LEE NAVIGATION - (London to Hertford) - Southern Volume.
68 pages, 33 photographs, 12 detailed maps and walks - walks between Limehouse Basin/River Thames and Enfield Lock. Includes Bow Creek River and City Mill Rivers. Includes 28 mile end to end walk - Limehouse Basin to Hertford.
Considerable History notes. ISBN 1-903627-74-5 £7.95 **NEW**

WALKING THE CANALS OF LONDON
End to End walks and circular walks on the Regent's Canal and Union Canal and the Paddington Branch, and exploraton of the Isle of Dogs and River Thames. Plus a London Canal Loop walk of 52 miles.
104 pages. 96 colour photographs. 18 maps. Wire Bound.
ISBN 978-0-9553691-2-4 £10.95 NEW

WALKING THE RIVER LEE NAVIGATION - 20 walks.
Both the South and North volumes in one book, plus additional walks around the 2012 Olympic Park area. ISBN 978-09553691-8-6 108 pages. Wire bound. £9.95 NEW

SHORT CIRCULAR WALKS IN THE COLNE VALLEY (Grand Union Canal) 8 walks - 3 to 11 miles long - that full eplore the area between Rickmansworth and Slough. One 20 mile walk - Rickmansworth to the River Thames.
72 pages. 12 maps. 40 photographs. ISBN 978-0-9560649-5-0 £7.95 NEW

WALKING THE CHELMER AND BLACKWATER NAVIGATION - 16 MILES - From Maldon to Chelmsford, Essex, beside this stunning and unspoilt waterway. NEW 2011

OTHER BOOKS by Revd. John N. Merrill

CIRCULAR WALK GUIDES -

SHORT CIRCULAR WALKS IN THE PEAK DISTRICT - Vols. 1 to 9
CIRCULAR WALKS IN WESTERN PEAKLAND
SHORT CIRCULAR WALKS IN THE STAFFORDSHIRE MOORLANDS
SHORT CIRCULAR WALKS - TOWNS & VILLAGES OF THE PEAK DISTRICT
SHORT CIRCULAR WALKS AROUND MATLOCK
SHORT CIRCULAR WALKS IN "PEAK PRACTICE COUNTRY."
SHORT CIRCULAR WALKS IN THE DUKERIES
SHORT CIRCULAR WALKS IN SOUTH YORKSHIRE
SHORT CIRCULAR WALKS IN SOUTH DERBYSHIRE
SHORT CIRCULAR WALKS AROUND BUXTON
SHORT CIRCULAR WALKS AROUND WIRKSWORTH
SHORT CIRCULAR WALKS IN THE HOPE VALLEY
40 SHORT CIRCULAR WALKS IN THE PEAK DISTRICT
CIRCULAR WALKS ON KINDER & BLEAKLOW
SHORT CIRCULAR WALKS IN SOUTH NOTTINGHAMSHIRE
SHORT CIRCULAR WALKS IN CHESHIRE
SHORT CIRCULAR WALKS IN WEST YORKSHIRE
WHITE PEAK DISTRICT AIRCRAFT WRECKS
CIRCULAR WALKS IN THE DERBYSHIRE DALES
SHORT CIRCULAR WALKS FROM BAKEWELL
SHORT CIRCULAR WALKS IN LATHKILL DALE
CIRCULAR WALKS IN THE WHITE PEAK
SHORT CIRCULAR WALKS IN EAST DEVON
SHORT CIRCULAR WALKS AROUND HARROGATE
SHORT CIRCULAR WALKS IN CHARNWOOD FOREST
SHORT CIRCULAR WALKS AROUND CHESTERFIELD
SHORT CIRCULAR WALKS IN THE YORKS DALES - Vol 1 - Southern area.
SHORT CIRCULAR WALKS IN THE AMBER VALLEY (Derbyshire)
SHORT CIRCULAR WALKS IN THE LAKE DISTRICT
SHORT CIRCULAR WALKS IN THE NORTH YORKSHIRE MOORS
SHORT CIRCULAR WALKS IN EAST STAFFORDSHIRE
LONG CIRCULAR WALKS IN THE PEAK DISTRICT - Vol.1 to 5.
DARK PEAK AIRCRAFT WRECK WALKS
LONG CIRCULAR WALKS IN THE STAFFORDSHIRE MOORLANDS
LONG CIRCULAR WALKS IN CHESHIRE
WALKING THE TISSINGTON TRAIL
WALKING THE HIGH PEAK TRAIL
WALKING THE MONSAL TRAIL & SETT VALLEY TRAILS
PEAK DISTRICT WALKING - TEN "TEN MILER'S" - Vol 1 and 2.
CLIMB THE PEAKS OF THE PEAK DISTRICT
PEAK DISTRICT WALK A MONTH Vols One, Two, Three, Four, Five & Six
TRAIN TO WALK Vol. One - The Hope Valley Line
DERBYSHIRE LOST VILLAGE WALKS -Vol One and Two.
CIRCULAR WALKS IN DOVEDALE AND THE MANIFOLD VALLEY
CIRCULAR WALKS AROUND GLOSSOP
WALKING THE LONGDENDALE TRAIL
WALKING THE UPPER DON TRAIL
SHORT CIRCULAR WALKS IN CANNOCK CHASE
CIRCULAR WALKS IN THE DERWENT VALLEY
WALKING THE TRAILS OF NORTH-EAST DERBYSHIRE
WALKING THE PENNINE BRIDLEWAY & CIRCULAR WALKS
SHORT CIRCULAR WALKS ON THE NEW RIVER & SOUTH-EAST HERTFORDSHIRE
SHORT CIRCULAR WALKS IN EPPING FOREST
SHORT CIRCULAR WALKS AROUND SAFFRON WALDEN
WALKING THE STREETS OF LONDON
LONG CIRCULAR WALKS IN EASTERN HERTFORDSHIRE
LONG CIRCULAR WALKS IN WESTERN HERTFORDSHIRE
WALKS IN THE LONDON BOROUGH OF ENFIELD
WALKS IN THE LONDON BOROUGH OF BARNET
WALKS IN THE LONDON BOROUGH OF HARINGEY
WALK IN THE LONDON BOROUGH OF WALTHAM FOREST
SHORT CIRCULAR WALKS AROUND HERTFORD
THE BIG WALKS OF LONDON
SHORT CIRCULAR WALKS AROUND BISHOP'S STORTFORD
SHORT CIRCULAR WALKS AROUND EPPING DISTRICT
CIRCULAR WALKS IN THE BOROUGH OF BROXBOURNE
LONDON INTERFAITH WALKS - Vol 1 and Vol. 2
LONG CIRCULAR WALKS IN THE NORTH CHILTERNS
SHORT CIRCULAR WALKS IN EASTERN HERTFORDSHIRE
WORCESTERSHIRE VILLAGE WALKS by Des Wright
WARWICKSHIRE VILLAGE WALKS by Des Wright
WALKING AROUND THE ROYAL PARKS OF LONDON
WALKS IN THE LONDON BOROUGH OF CHELSEA AND ROYAL KENSINGTON

CANAL WALKS -

VOL 1 - DERBYSHIRE & NOTTINGHAMSHIRE
VOL 2 - CHESHIRE & STAFFORDSHIRE
VOL 3 - STAFFORDSHIRE
VOL 4 - THE CHESHIRE RING
VOL 5 - THE GRANTHAM CANAL
VOL 6 - SOUTH YORKSHIRE
VOL 7 - THE TRENT & MERSEY CANAL
VOL 8 - WALKING THE DERBY CANAL RING
VOL 9 - WALKING THE LLANGOLLEN CANAL
VOL 10 - CIRCULAR WALKS ON THE CHESTERFIELD CANAL
VOL 11 - CIRCULAR WALKS ON THE CROMFORD CANAL
Vol.13 - SHORT CIRCULAR WALKS ON THE RIVER LEE NAVIGATION -Vol. 1 - North
Vol. 14 - SHORT CIRCULAR WALKS ON THE RIVER STORT NAVIGATION
Vol.15 - SHORT CIRCULAR WALKS ON THE RIVER LEE NAVIGATION - Vol. 2 - South
Vol. 16 - WALKING THE CANALS OF LONDON
Vol 17 - WALKING THE RIVER LEE NAVIGATION
Vol. 20 - SHORT CIRCULAR WALKS IN THE COLNE VALLEY
Vol 21 - THE BLACKWATER & CHELMER NAVIGATION - End to End.
Vol. 22 - NOTTINGHAM'S LOST CANAL by Bernard Chell.
Vol. 23 - WALKING THE RIVER WEY & GODALMING NAVIAGTIONS END TO END
Vol.25 - WALKING THE GRAND UNION CANAL - LONDON TO BIRMINGHAM.

JOHN MERRILL DAY CHALLENGE WALKS

WHITE PEAK CHALLENGE WALK
THE HAPPY HIKER - WHITE PEAK - CHALLENGE WALK
DARK PEAK CHALLENGE WALK
PEAK DISTRICT END TO END WALKS
STAFFORDSHIRE MOORLANDS CHALLENGE WALK

JOHN MERRILL DAY CHALLENGE WALKS

WHITE PEAK CHALLENGE WALK
THE HAPPY HIKER - WHITE PEAK - CHALLENGE WALK No.2
DARK PEAK CHALLENGE WALK
PEAK DISTRICT END TO END WALKS
STAFFORDSHIRE MOORLANDS CHALLENGE WALK
THE LITTLE JOHN CHALLENGE WALK
YORKSHIRE DALES CHALLENGE WALK
NORTH YORKSHIRE MOORS CHALLENGE WALK
LAKELAND CHALLENGE WALK
THE RUTLAND WATER CHALLENGE WALK
MALVERN HILLS CHALLENGE WALK
THE SALTERIS WAY
THE SNOWDON CHALLENGE
CHARNWOOD FOREST CHALLENGE WALK
THREE COUNTIES CHALLENGE WALK (Peak District).
CAL-DER-WENT WALK
THE QUANTOCK WAY
BELVOIR WITCHES CHALLENGE WALK
THE CARNEDDAU CHALLENGE WALK
THE SWEET PEA CHALLENGE WALK
THE LINCOLNSHIRE WOLDS - BLACK DEATH - CHALLENGE WALK
JENNIFER'S CHALLENGE WALK
THE EPPING FOREST CHALLENGE WALK
THE THREE BOROUGH CHALLENGE WALK - NORTH LONDON
THE HERTFORD CHALLENGE WALK
THE BOSHAM CHALLENGE WALK
THE KING JOHN CHALLENGE WALK
THE NORFOLK BROADS CHALLENGE WALK
THE RIVER MIMRAM WALK
THE ISLE OF THANET CHHALENGE WALK

INSTRUCTION & RECORD -

HIKE TO BE FIT.....STROLLING WITH JOHN
THE JOHN MERRILL WALK RECORD BOOK
HIKE THE WORLD - John Merrill's guide to walking & Backpacking.

MULTIPLE DAY WALKS -

THE RIVERS'S WAY
PEAK DISTRICT: HIGH LEVEL ROUTE
PEAK DISTRICT MARATHONS
THE LIMEY WAY
THE PEAKLAND WAY
COMPO'S WAY by Alan Hiley
THE BRIGHTON WAY

COAST WALKS & NATIONAL TRAILS -

ISLE OF WIGHT COAST PATH
PEMBROKESHIRE COAST PATH
THE CLEVELAND WAY
WALKING ANGELSEY'S COASTLINE.
WALKING THE COASTLINE OF THE CHANNEL ISLANDS
THE ISLE OF MAN COASTAL PATH - "The Way of the Gull."
A WALK AROUND HAYLING ISLAND
A WALK AROUND THE ISLE OF SHEPPEY
A WALK AROUND THE ISLE OF JERSEY
WALKING AROUND THE ISLANDS OF ESSEX

DERBYSHIRE & PEAK DISTRICT HISTORICAL GUIDES -

A to Z GUIDE OF THE PEAK DISTRICT
DERBYSHIRE INNS - an A to Z guide
HALLS AND CASTLES OF THE PEAK DISTRICT & DERBYSHIRE
TOURING THE PEAK DISTRICT & DERBYSHIRE BY CAR
DERBYSHIRE FOLKLORE
PUNISHMENT IN DERBYSHIRE
CUSTOMS OF THE PEAK DISTRICT & DERBYSHIRE
WINSTER - a souvenir guide
ARKWRIGHT OF CROMFORD
LEGENDS OF DERBYSHIRE
DERBYSHIRE FACTS & RECORDS
TALES FROM THE MINES by Geoffrey Carr
PEAK DISTRICT PLACE NAMES by Martin Spray
DERBYSHIRE THROUGH THE AGES - Vol 1 -DERBYSHIRE IN PREHISTORIC TIMES
SIR JOSEPH PAXTON
FLORENCE NIGHTINGALE
JOHN SMEDLEY
BONNIE PRINCE CHARLIE & 20 mile walk.
THE STORY OF THE EARLS AND DUKES OF DEVONSHIRE

JOHN MERRILL'S MAJOR WALKS -

TURN RIGHT AT LAND'S END
WITH MUSTARD ON MY BACK
TURN RIGHT AT DEATH VALLEY
EMERALD COAST WALK
I CHOSE TO WALK - Why I walk etc.
A WALK IN OHIO - 1,310 miles around the Buckeye Trail.
I AM GUIDED - the story of John's wal;king life.

SKETCH BOOKS -

SKETCHES OF THE PEAK DISTRICT

COLOUR BOOK:-

THE PEAK DISTRICT.......something to remember her by.

OVERSEAS GUIDES -

HIKING IN NEW MEXICO - Vol I - The Sandia and Manzano Mountains.
Vol 2 - Hiking "Billy the Kid" Country.
Vol 4 - N.W. area - " Hiking Indian Country."
"WALKING IN DRACULA COUNTRY" - Romania.
WALKING THE TRAILS OF THE HONG KONG ISLANDS.

VISITOR GUIDES - MATLOCK . BAKEWELL. ASHBOURNE.

See all my books on -
www.johnmerrillwalkguides.co.uk

Pilgrim Guides -
www.thejohnmerrillministry.co.uk

COMPANION CANAL GUIDES -

SHORT CIRCULAR WALKS ON THE CROMFORD CANAL by John N. Merrill

THE DERBYSHIRE CANAL WALKS SERIES - Vol Two

SHORT CIRCULAR WALKS ON THE CROMFORD CANAL

by John N. Merrill

Eleven circular walks on the Cromford Canal, berween Cromford and Langley Mill.

WALKING THE DERBY CANAL RING

by John N. Merrill

Walk the Derby Ring - 28 miles - following the line of the Derby Canal and the Trent & Mersey and Erewash Canals. The successful can obtain a special embroidered badge and signed certificate.

Walk the Trent & Mersey Canal End to End - a magnificent level 100 mile walk from Runcorn, Cheshire to Shardlow, Derbyshire. The successful can obtain a special badge and signed certificate.

Twenty walks exploring the full length of this unique canal from Chesterfield to West Stockwith and the River Trent.

15 short circular walks on the Grantham Canal,
between the River Trent and Grantham;
through the Vale of Belvoir.
- the hidden walking area of the East Midlands!

OTHER PEAK DISTRICT & DERBYSHIRE BOOKS by Revd. John N. Merrill

CIRCULAR WALK GUIDES -

SHORT CIRCULAR WALKS IN THE PEAK DISTRICT - Vols. 1 to 9
CIRCULAR WALKS IN WESTERN PEAKLAND
SHORT CIRCULAR WALKS IN THE STAFFORDSHIRE MOORLANDS
SHORT CIRCULAR WALKS - TOWNS & VILLAGES OF THE PEAK DISTRICT
SHORT CIRCULAR WALKS AROUND MATLOCK
SHORT CIRCULAR WALKS IN "PEAK PRACTICE COUNTRY."
SHORT CIRCULAR WALKS IN SOUTH DERBYSHIRE
SHORT CIRCULAR WALKS AROUND BUXTON
SHORT CIRCULAR WALKS AROUND WIRKSWORTH
SHORT CIRCULAR WALKS IN THE HOPE VALLEY
40 SHORT CIRCULAR WALKS IN THE PEAK DISTRICT
CIRCULAR WALKS ON KINDER & BLEAKLOW
WHITE PEAK DISTRICT AIRCRAFT WRECKS
CIRCULAR WALKS IN THE DERBYSHIRE DALES
SHORT CIRCULAR WALKS FROM BAKEWELL
SHORT CIRCULAR WALKS IN LATHKILL DALE
CIRCULAR WALKS IN THE WHITE PEAK
SHORT CIRCULAR WALKS AROUND CHESTERFIELD
SHORT CIRCULAR WALKS IN THE AMBER VALLEY (Derbyshire)
SHORT CIRCULAR WALKS IN EAST STAFFORDSHIRE
LONG CIRCULAR WALKS IN THE PEAK DISTRICT - Vol.1 to 5.
DARK PEAK AIRCRAFT WRECK WALKS
LONG CIRCULAR WALKS IN THE STAFFORDSHIRE MOORLANDS
LONG CIRCULAR WALKS IN CHESHIRE
WALKING THE TISSINGTON TRAIL
WALKING THE HIGH PEAK TRAIL
WALKING THE MONSAL TRAIL & SETT VALLEY TRAILS
PEAK DISTRICT WALKING - TEN "TEN MILER'S" - Vol 1 and 2.
CLIMB THE PEAKS OF THE PEAK DISTRICT
PEAK DISTRICT WALK A MONTH Vols One,Two, Three, Four, Five & Six
TRAIN TO WALK Vol. One - The Hope Valley Line
DERBYSHIRE LOST VILLAGE WALKS -Vol One and Two.
CIRCULAR WALKS IN DOVEDALE AND THE MANIFOLD VALLEY
CIRCULAR WALKS AROUND GLOSSOP
WALKING THE LONGDENDALE TRAIL
WALKING THE UPPER DON TRAIL
CIRCULAR WALKS IN THE DERWENT VALLEY
WALKING THE TRAILS OF NORTH-EAST DERBYSHIRE
WALKING THE PENNINE BRIDLEWAY & CIRCULAR WALKS

CANAL WALKS -

VOL 1 - DERBYSHIRE & NOTTINGHAMSHIRE
VOL 3 - STAFFORDSHIRE
VOL 8 - WALKING THE DERBY CANAL RING
VOL 10 - CIRCULAR WALKS ON THE CHESTERFIELD CANAL
VOL 11 - CIRCULAR WALKS ON THE CROMFORD CANAL

JOHN MERRILL DAY CHALLENGE WALKS

WHITE PEAK CHALLENGE WALK No. 1
THE HAPPY HIKER - WHITE PEAK - CHALLENGE WALK No. 2
DARK PEAK CHALLENGE WALK
PEAK DISTRICT END TO END WALKS
STAFFORDSHIRE MOORLANDS CHALLENGE WALK
THREE COUNTIES CHALLENGE WALK

INSTRUCTION & RECORD -

HIKE TO BE FIT.....STROLLING WITH JOHN
THE JOHN MERRILL WALK RECORD BOOK
HIKE THE WORLD - John Merrill's guide to walking & Backpacking.

MULTIPLE DAY WALKS -

THE RIVERS'S WAY
PEAK DISTRICT: HIGH LEVEL ROUTE
PEAK DISTRICT MARATHONS
THE LIMEY WAY
THE PEAKLAND WAY
COMPO'S WAY by Alan Hiley
CAL-DER-WENT WALK

DERBYSHIRE & PEAK DISTRICT HISTORICAL GUIDES -

A to Z GUIDE OF THE PEAK DISTRICT
DERBYSHIRE INNS - an A to Z guide
HALLS AND CASTLES OF THE PEAK DISTRICT & DERBYSHIRE
TOURING THE PEAK DISTRICT & DERBYSHIRE BY CAR
DERBYSHIRE FOLKLORE
PUNISHMENT IN DERBYSHIRE
CUSTOMS OF THE PEAK DISTRICT & DERBYSHIRE
WINSTER - a souvenir guide
ARKWRIGHT OF CROMFORD
LEGENDS OF DERBYSHIRE
DERBYSHIRE FACTS & RECORDS
TALES FROM THE MINES by Geoffrey Carr
PEAK DISTRICT PLACE NAMES by Martin Spray
DERBYSHIRE THROUGH THE AGES - Vol 1 - DERBYSHIRE IN PREHISTORIC TIMES
SIR JOSEPH PAXTON
FLORENCE NIGHTINGALE
JOHN SMEDLEY
BONNIE PRINCE CHARLIE & 20 mile walk.
THE STORY OF THE EARLS AND DUKES OF DEVONSHIRE
DERBYSHIRE PILGRIMAGE

SKETCH BOOKS -

SKETCHES OF THE PEAK DISTRICT

COLOUR BOOK -

THE PEAK DISTRICT.......something to remember her by.

VISITOR GUIDES -

MATLOCK .
BAKEWELL.
ASHBOURNE.

See all my books on - www.johnmerrillwalkguides.co.uk

Pilgrim Guides - www.thejohnmerrillministry.co.uk

Follow the Countryside Code.

* Be safe - plan ahead and follow any signs.

* Leave gates and property as you find them.

* Protect plants and animals, and take your litter home.

* Keep dogs under close control.

* Consider other people.

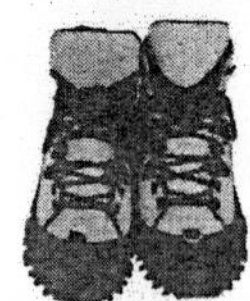

EQUIPMENT NOTES
.... some personal thoughts -

Today there is a bewildering variety of walking gear, much is superfluous to general walking in Britain. As a basic observation, people over dress for the outdoors. Basically equipment should be serviceable and do the task. I don't use walking poles; humans were built to walk with two legs! The following are some of my thoughts gathered from my walking experiences.

BOOTS - For summer use and day walking I wear lightweight boots. For high mountains and longer trips I prefer a good quality boot with a full leather upper, of medium weight, traditional style ,with a vibram sole. I always add a foam cushioned insole to help cushion the base of my feet.

SOCKS - I generally wear two thick pairs as this helps minimise blisters. The inner pair are of loop stitch variety and approximately 80% wool. The outer are also a thick pair of approximately 80% wool. I often wear double inner socks, which minimise blisters.

CLOTHES & WATERPROOFS - for general walking I wear a T shirt or cotton shirt with a cotton wind jacket on top, and shorts - even in snow! You generate heat as you walk and I prefer to layer my clothes to avoid getting too hot. Depending on the season will dictate how many layers you wear. In soft rain I just use my wind jacket for I know it quickly dries out. In heavy or consistent rain I slip on a poncho, which covers me and my pack and allows air to circulate, while keeping me dry. Only in extreme conditions will I don over-trousers, much preferring to get wet and feel comfortable. I never wear gaiters, except when cross country skiing, or in snow and glacier crossings. I find running shorts and sleeveless T shirts ideal for summer.

FOOD - as I walk I carry bars of chocolate, for they provide instant energy and are light to carry. In winter a flask of hot coffee is welcome. I never carry water and find no hardship from not doing so, but this is a personal matter and how indivudual bodies work! From experience I find the more I drink the more I want and sweat. You should always carry some extra food such as trail mix & candy bars etc., for emergencies. Full milk is a very underestimated source of food and liquid.

RUCKSACKS - for day walking I use a rucksack of about 20/30 litre capacity and although it leaves excess space it does mean that the sac is well padded, with an internal frame and padded shoulder straps, chest strap and waist strap. Inside apart from the basics for one day, in winter I carry gloves, wear a hat/cap and carry a spare pullover and a pair of socks.

MAP & COMPASS - when I am walking I always have the relevant map - preferably 1:25,000 scale - open in my hand. This enables me to constantly check that I am walking the right way. In case of bad weather I carry a compass, which once mastered gives you complete confidence in thick cloud or mist - you should always know where you are; I have a built in direction finder! Map reading and compass work is a skill and should be learnt. With modern technology you can now downloaded OS maps to your phone, record your walk - mileage, calories used, steps taken, walking speed and time taken.

WHY I WALK *by Revd. John N. Merrill*

I walk for the exercise; to stretch my legs and muscles; to suck in the fresh air and be free in the wide, wide world, as I walk upon Mother Earth.

I walk to see the trees; that sway in the breeze. To watch the leaves flutter in summer and to walk through on the ground in November. I observe the quietness of winter and watch the buds form ready to emerge when it is their time.

I walk to see the wild flowers; the wood anemones, the blue bells, red campion, and orchids that grow in Spring and early summer.

I walk to listen to the birds that sing in the hedgerows and trees. The friendly Robin is not far away, the started Jay or motionless heron standing at the waters edge. A sudden flash of blue as a kingfisher shoots by.

I walk to see the wild animals; the red fox, the deer, the squirrel and the insects and butterflies, like the dragonfly and red admiral butterfly.

I walk to see the views; to ascend a lofty peak and sit upon the summit surveying everything below, like an eagle high in the air.

I walk for solitude; peace and quiet, to go back to the basics of life, where it is just man and the elements.

I walk in the sunshine, the rain, snow and wind. All has its own beauty and characteristic. All are the cycles of life. I admire the cloudless sky and the rolling clouds of wind and storm.

I walk to see the work of man and God, knowing that we are all connected. Everything has its own beauty.

As the sun sets and I walk home, I know I have lived and experienced a full day, witnessing the whole spectrum of life. I am grateful, very grateful, that God gave me two fine legs, a healthy heart and good lungs to see paradise on Earth.

HOW TO DO A WALK

The walks in this book follow public right of ways, be it a footpath, bridleway, Boat or Rupp. which are marked on the Ordnance Survey 1:25,000 Explorer Series of maps.

On each walk I have detailed which map are needed and I would urge you to carry and use a map. As I walk I always have the map out on the section I am walking, constantly checking that I am walking the right way. Also when coming to any road or path junction, I can check on the map to ensure I take the right route.

Most paths are signed and waymarked with coloured arrows - yellow for footpaths; blue for bridleways - but I would at best describe them as intermittent. They act as confirmation of the right of way you are walking and the arrow usually point in the direction of travel.

The countryside has the added problem of vandalism and you will find path logo's and Information Boards spray painted over and even path signs pointing the wrong way! That is why I always advise carrying the map open on the area you are walking to check you are walking the right way. In my walking instructions I have given the name and number of each main and minor road, canal lock and bridge number, together with house numbers where you turn and the name of the inns passed. Wherever I add what the footpath sign says, plus the stiles, footbridges and kissing gates en route. All to help you have a smooth and trouble free walk.

I confirm that I have walked every route and written what I found at the time of walking.

Most people don't walk correctly with a straight spine and feet parallel to each other, and a few inches apart. Each step starts the cycle of lifting the foot a little way off the ground and placing the heel down first, then moving forward as the foot bends with the toes being last to leave the ground as the cycle begins again. It is all a gentle fluid rolling motion; with practice you can glide across the terrain, effortlessly, for mile after mile.

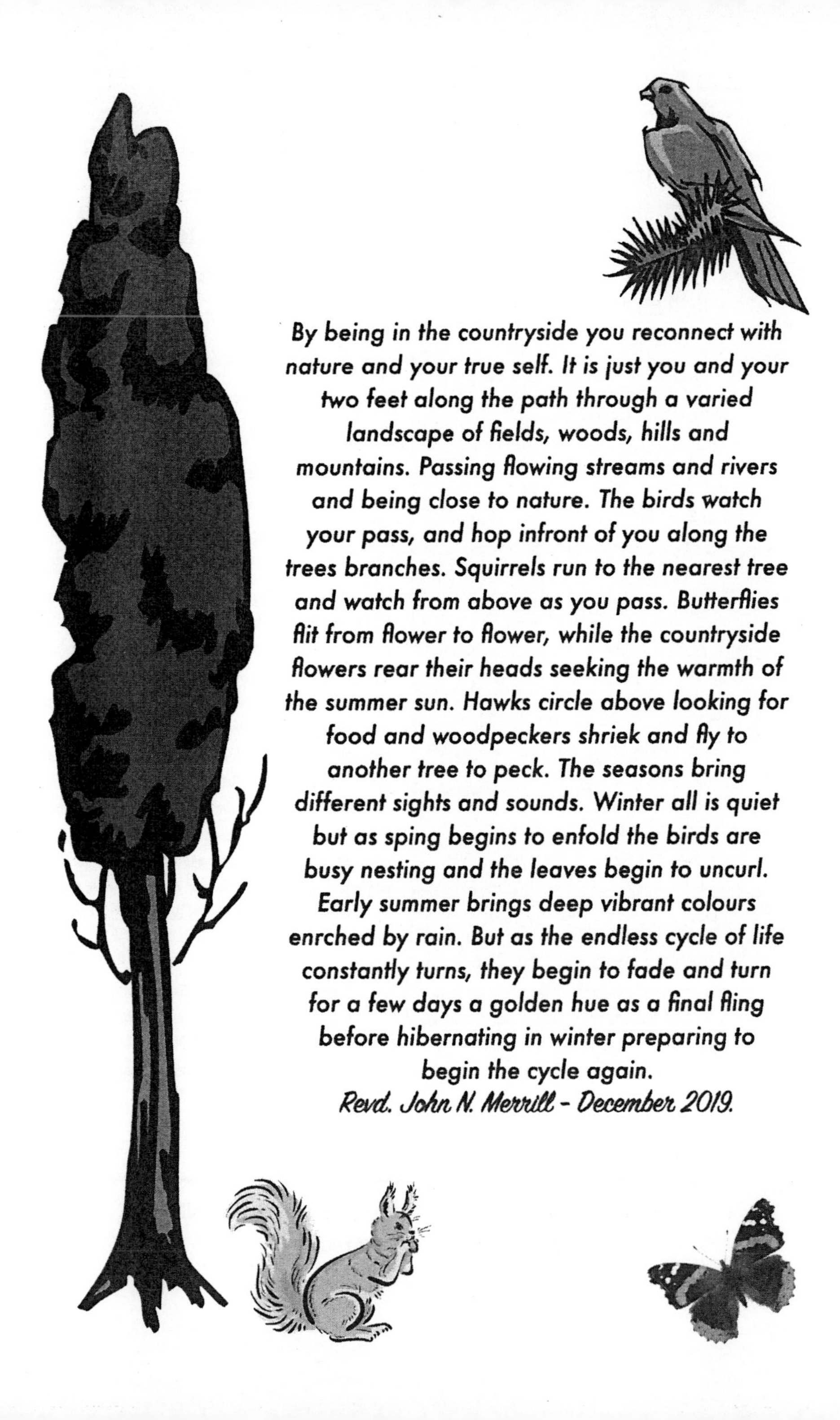

By being in the countryside you reconnect with nature and your true self. It is just you and your two feet along the path through a varied landscape of fields, woods, hills and mountains. Passing flowing streams and rivers and being close to nature. The birds watch your pass, and hop infront of you along the trees branches. Squirrels run to the nearest tree and watch from above as you pass. Butterflies flit from flower to flower, while the countryside flowers rear their heads seeking the warmth of the summer sun. Hawks circle above looking for food and woodpeckers shriek and fly to another tree to peck. The seasons bring different sights and sounds. Winter all is quiet but as sping begins to enfold the birds are busy nesting and the leaves begin to uncurl. Early summer brings deep vibrant colours enrched by rain. But as the endless cycle of life constantly turns, they begin to fade and turn for a few days a golden hue as a final fling before hibernating in winter preparing to begin the cycle again.

Revd. John N. Merrill - December 2019.

Revd. John N. Merrill
HonMuniv
Funeral Celebrant, Weddings, Ashes Internment, Sermons, Talks & Pilgrimages.
Multi-Faith Minister

"Embracing and honouring all faiths and none, and all nationalities."

John has been following his own unique spiritual path all his life and is guided and looked after. He was brought up a Christian and confirmed at the age of 11. He went to a Quaker Boarding school for five years and developed his love of the countryside and outdoors. He became fascinated with Tibet and whilst retaining his Christian roots, became immersed in Buddhism, later spending four years at the Tara Buddhist Centre in Derbyshire. He now encorporates Taoism and attends the Chinese Buddhist Centre in London. With his thirst for knowledge and discovery he paid attention to other faiths and appreciated their teachings and values. Late in life he decided it was time to reveal his spiritual beliefs and practices and discovered the Interfaith Seminary.

Here for two years he learnt in more depth the whole spectrum of faiths, including Jainism, Paganism, Mother Earth, Buddhism, Hinduism, Islam, Judaism, Sikhism, Celtic Worship and Shamanism. This is an ongoing exploration without end. All faiths have their own beauty and path. All lead to the same destination. He was ordained on July 17th. 2010 as an multi-faith Minister and Spiritual Counsellor. He has now done more than 500 funeral services and numerous weddings, including one in Sarajevo, Bosnia.

"May you go in peace, with joy in your heart
and may the divine be always at your side."

THE JOHN MERRILL MINISTRY, Enfield, London. EN8 8QY
Email - marathonhiker@aol.com
Tel. 01992 762776